THE MODERN PUBLIC SECTOR

THE MODERN PUBLIC SECTOR

NEW WAYS OF DOING
THE GOVERNMENT'S BUSINESS

Murray L. Weidenbaum

Basic Books, Inc., Publishers | New York | London

FOREWORD

The treatment of the public sector by many economists, particularly in preparing textbooks in public finance, brings to mind images of thousands and thousands of clerks working in innumerable bureaus and agencies who, on occasion, purchase pens, pencils, paper, desks, and chairs from private firms. An aside or a few footnotes may remind the reader that this simple environment is on occasion interrupted by wars and similar crises, and more "up-to-date" authors have even begun to take account of the growing volume of dams, buildings, and other government construction projects since the 1930's. But, by and large, the basic analysis remains pure enough.

The main purpose of this book is to demonstrate that this idyllic picture of the public sector does not conform to the realities of twentieth-century America, if it ever did earlier. The civil service clerk preparing innocuous reports that are to be duplicated, filed, and refiled, although a stock figure of dramatic fiction, represents a trivial case of public resource utilization.

Today, the federal government, as a user of resources, is primarily an agency of military preparation and, secondarily, of scientific exploration, economic development, and social welfare experimentation and amelioration. Of the $60 billion of federal government purchases of goods and services from the private sector each year, approximately one-half consists of items designed, developed, and produced under close government supervision—weapon systems such as aircraft, missiles, tanks, ships, and artillery. The great bulk of the remainder is purchased to operate and maintain the weapons, such as fuel, lubricants, and necessities (food, clothing, shelter) for the members of the armed forces using them. Purchases of goods and services by civilian agencies of the federal government—consisting mainly of standard commercial items such as office equipment and medical supplies —come to $10 billion for a year or less than one-fifth of the total.

When viewed as a whole, the modern public sector, as it has developed in the United States, is characterized by (1) a widespread reliance upon government-oriented corporations and other quasi-private organizations that perform government functions under close surveillance; (2) a massive use of advanced research concepts and high technology; (3) shifting relationships between federal and state governments, with more of the funds coming from the former and more of the end activities performed by the latter; and (4) government expansion into areas for which traditional public agencies are not well equipped but in which private markets do not exist to any significant degree.

The rise of the government-oriented private corporation is a different development from what has historically been encountered in a "mixed" public and private economy. Unlike, say, the generation and distribution of power where, at some location, the work is done by government agencies such as the Tennessee Valley Authority and, in other places, by private corporations, we are here dealing with the intermingling of public and private authority within the same business corporation. Here the question often is how much of the internal policies and operations of these corporations is determined by private management and how much by government officials.

The quasi-private organization, nominally a nonprofit research or eleemosynary institution which obtains the bulk of its funds from the federal government, represents a further blend between the public and the private agency.

In a fundamental sense, the dividing line between the public and the private sectors is shifting. The federal government is taking on functions that have often been performed elsewhere, at least in the past, and private organizations increasingly are being oriented to serving governmental, rather than private, customers or clients. The development of this new type of public sector is already having an important impact in many specific areas of the economy and of society generally. The many recommendations to extend this close public-private relationship to other areas, such as urban transportation, welfare, and so forth, make it especially important to evaluate the economic and political implications of these trends. That is what this book hopes to do.

ACKNOWLEDGMENTS

The author acknowledges an indirect debt to his colleagues in the Department of Economics at Washington University for creating the type of environment in which relatively untraditional, interdisciplinary work could be conducted in a favorable atmosphere. Parts of this volume draw upon research performed by the author under NASA Grant NGR 26–008–003 to Washington University.

Portions of Chapter 2 and 6 have appeared, in earlier form, in the *American Economic Review*, the *National Tax Journal*, and the *Quarterly Review of Economics and Business;* the editors have kindly consented to the use of some of these materials.

CONTENTS

THE MODERN PUBLIC SECTOR

1

FUNDAMENTAL CHANGES IN
THE PUBLIC SECTOR

Public attention to government activities usually focuses on ephemeral issues such as the size of the budget deficit, the expansion of the national debt, or the excessive purchases of oyster forks or paper blankets. On more serious occasions, taxpayers and other interested citizens are concerned with the important developments of the day: Should the nation embark upon a massive anti-poverty program? Should we subsidize the development of a supersonic airliner? Should a major effort be made to reduce air and water pollution?

Yet the most fundamental developments in the role of government in the United States are deeper than either of these kinds of issues. While they lack the humor of the uncovered goof by a public official or the dramatic aspects of the "burning issue of the day," they exert a strong influence on both the kinds of activities which government undertakes and on the effectiveness with which these functions are performed. For when we probe more deeply, we find that several basic changes are taking place in the nature of the public sector and in the structure of governmental institutions.

The transcending, but undramatic, development that has been

3

occurring in the structure of the American public sector is the intermingling between public and private activities and between federal government and state-local governmental operations to the point where the dividing line between the federal government's sphere of operations and the rest of the economy has become increasingly blurred, if not eliminated. As we shall see, the simplistic notion of a public sector of government officials and clerks dealing with a private sector of business firms needs to be updated to reflect a far more complex and subtle array of relationships, both *within* the public sector and *between* the public and private sectors.

The basic cause of these changes can be traced to a growing division in governmental functions between policy formulation and supervision, on the one hand, and actual program execution on the other. Primarily, but of course not entirely, the agencies of the federal government, both legislative and executive, have been designing and developing policies concerning the national defense, welfare, and economic growth, appropriating funds for achieving these policies, and also overseeing and reviewing the results. However, the execution of these policies—the actual production of public goods and services—has in large measure and on an increasing scale been delegated or contracted out to organizations outside of the federal government. Some of these organizations are within the public sector itself; many others are lodged in the private sector.

The variety of institutional alternatives is made available by using a combination of contracts and grants-in-aid to involve private industry, state and local governments, and nonprofit institutions in the federal government's activities. These different institutional arrangements all share a single characteristic. They are all responses to a common set of problems facing our society as a whole and, hence, our national government.

Despite internal developmental efforts (discussed later in this chapter), the in-house managerial, administrative, and production resources available to the federal government are not sufficient to cope with the combined tasks of carrying on the traditional public activities and simultaneously assuming an almost bewildering array of new or greatly expanded functions. The most dramatic examples of the latter include designing and producing a vast arsenal of technologically sophisticated weapon and space systems, building and operating a nationwide air and surface transportation network, conducting a crash effort to reduce the incidence of poverty, establishing an innovative educational research effort in each region of the country, and processing and adjudicating millions of Medicare claims a year. By all indications, there is more to come.

The shift in the location of the actual conduct of government programs gives rise to more than just administrative and managerial repercussions. It strongly influences the role of the states and cities in our federal form of government. It affects the size and strength of the business sector and of other nongovernmental institutions in our economy which has been primarily geared to corporate enterprise and private initiative.

But, overriding all of these effects, the contracting-out and delegation of the execution of government programs is altering the basic nature of the public sector of the United States. Moreover, this change introduces another aspect of decision-making into the formulation of government programs. Not only do choices have to be made between specific program areas (that is, to put additional funds into education or health), but basic aspects of governmental decisions now involve selecting the mechanism through which the government will act to achieve its objectives.

The question is no longer, "which government agency should be assigned the new program?" Rather, the problem has been broadened to include such options as setting up new federal agencies or drawing on existing expertise outside of the federal government. If the latter route is chosen, another set of questions then comes to the fore: "Should the states be involved, via grants-in-aid?" or "Should private industry be assigned to the actual administration through business contracts negotiated between the corporation and the government?"

If the governmental policy-maker is not satisfied with existing institutions, he can now consider either establishing a new federal agency to conduct the program or encouraging the formation of a nonprofit institution which, at least legally, is located in the private sector of the economy.

Thus, a decision to embark upon a new program to reduce air pollution may also involve decisions concerning the role of the states, the size of the government "market" available to private industry, the organizational structure of the federal establishment and, perhaps, the opportunity to expand the third (or nonprofit) sector of our society. The present is clearly an exploratory period in the development of the institutional structure of the American public sector. Many different types of mechanisms are being experimented with. The resultant economic and related public policy implications are both varied and substantial. Peter Drucker, a distinguished student of management, has offered "the main lesson of the last fifty years: government is not a 'doer.'" The purpose of government, Professor Drucker states, is "to make fundamental decisions . . . to govern." But, he concludes somewhat arbitrarily, "This, as we have learned in other institutions, is incompatible with 'doing.' Any attempt to combine government with 'doing' on a large scale paralyzes the decision-making capacity."[1]

A balanced appraisal of American governmental institutions in modern times would, I think, reveal some truth as well as considerable overstatement in Drucker's argument. But before we can make such an appraisal we shall have to examine the institutional changes in the conduct of public programs, and the motivations for making such changes.

The Size of the Managerial Task

It is therefore important that we examine the reasons for and causes of the growing specialization of labor in the public sector of the United States and the different ways in which the various government agencies have responded. One clear and apparent reason for the delegation of duties by the federal government is the sheer size of the job. No longer is the government's role limited to that of merely providing basic protection, for example, police, defense, and a limited monitoring of the marketplace through antitrust, fraud laws, and so forth. In many ways, government today is charged with ultimate responsibility for the employment and the basic welfare of the citizenry. As a result, it has become involved in more pervasive regulatory functions, such as monetary and fiscal policy and the promulgation of wage-price norms, as well as inauguration of vast programs for investing in human resources.

Significantly, government at all levels is currently expending at a rate of $285 billion a year. This compares with a national income of $712 billion a year. Thus government expenditure is equal to approximately 40 per cent of the total national income. Even taking into account the fact that government expenditures are not entirely reflected in national income, the ratio is impressive. Government purchases of goods and services are running at $200 billion a year, which means that government claims almost 25 per cent of the Gross National Product (GNP) which is now at $860 billion annually.[2] Such a vast expenditure naturally has tremendous importance for the economy.

Another way of considering the relative size of the federal establishment is to compare its component parts with units in the other parts of the economy. For example, the contrast between the largest department of government and the private business firms with the highest sales volumes is instructive: the annual expenditures of the Department of Defense alone are equal to the combined yearly sales of five of the largest industrial firms in the United States—General Motors, Standard Oil of New Jersey, Ford, General Electric, and Chrysler. The annual expenditures of the National Aeronautics and Space Administration (NASA) are roughly the same as the budget of the state of New York. When we look beyond the borders of the United States, we find still other confirmation of the mammoth size of the federal government. The yearly disbursements by the Veterans Administration alone are greater than those of the national government of Belgium!

Decentralization of governmental activities at the state level is historic and well known. The bulk of state and local taxes is raised and spent by local units (cities, towns, counties, school boards, special fire and sewer districts) which are legally creatures of the state. The annual expenditures by the municipal government of the city of New York alone are larger than those of the state government of New York.[3]

When we examine large organizations in the private sector, we find them also facing grave problems of management of diversified, far-flung operations. The giants of American industry, and even many smaller firms, continually report new efforts to decentralize and otherwise reorganize their operations to deal more effectively and efficiently with the many varied managerial and project considerations that arise. So-called profit or burden centers are scattered throughout many of these corporations in order to give a large number of managers within a given corporation a sense of primary responsibility for a piece of the total enterprise.

The tale is told that a vice-president of General Electric asked a banker friend of his to introduce him to the President of General Electric as he had never met him personally. Perhaps the tale is mythical. However, the extent to which private organizations struggle with problems of internal communications and control is indicative of the difficulties in dealing with the management requirements of large-scale operations. The managerial problems facing the federal government are on a larger scale than those of any other public or private organization, perhaps by several orders of magnitude.

In addition, the federal government faces further complexities of a qualitative nature. As it takes on further functions, it requires new products and new services for which there are few precedents or established markets. The governmental "market basket" is a strange and rapidly changing one. The products it purchases vary from ICBM's to nuclear-powered aircraft carriers, space vehicles, and salt and brackish water purification systems. The services it requires are more challenging still—poverty reduction, environmental pollution control, beautification, and urban renewal.

Thus, the federal government faces an increasingly difficult task of managing a highly technical, widely diversified, and rapidly growing enterprise without being able to rely upon useful precedents.

The Rise of the New Contracting-Out Agencies

The federal government's tendency to become primarily a policy formulator and overseer is most clearly seen when we examine the nature of the most recently established departments and programs. In virtually every case, the agencies created during the past two decades possess characteristics differing from those of the traditional federal departments and activities; they typify the trend toward a new "contractual" public sector.

Old-line agencies typically devote the great bulk of their resources to their own payroll and direct operations. The Treasury Department devotes nine-tenths of its budget to wages and salaries aside from interest payments on the national debt. The Post Office, for example, has the largest work force of any civilian agency because it relies on its own letter carriers to deliver the mails; its employment costs account for over three-fourths of its budget. The Justice Department budget is assigned primarily to pay the lawyers, investigators, border patrol agents, and prison guards working for its various bureaus and offices. Likewise, the State Department budget goes mainly for salary and related payments to the Foreign Service officers and other government personnel who are involved in the conduct of foreign relations.

In contrast, the Department of Health, Education, and Welfare (HEW), created in 1953, makes well over nine-tenths of its expenditures in the form of grants-in-aid to state and local governments and transfer payments to individuals. Although large in absolute size, its own payroll represents only 6 per cent of its total budget. The National Aeronautics and Space Administration (NASA), established in 1958, spends nine-tenths of its budget on contracts with private industry, universities, and research institutes; it is these private organizations that do most of the actual space research and development work that the agency sponsors. NASA employees primarily monitor and review the contractor efforts and, of course, actually utilize the satellites and other space vehicles that are produced.

The anti-poverty program under the Office of Economic Opportunity (OEO), set up in 1964, operates primarily through programs which it finances but which are conducted by organizations outside of the federal establishment. Some of these are units of state and local governments; others are private corporations. Many others are nonprofit organizations set up in the private sector especially to administer the federal funds. Similarly, the Department of Housing and Urban Development, established in 1965, operates with a relatively small work force of its own, also accounting for about one-tenth of its disbursements. The department's employees primarily make or supervise loans, grants-in-aid, and other financial assistance to state and local governments; it is the latter who are actually carrying out the programs in the department's area of interest. The most recently established federal agency, the Department of Transportation, formed in 1966, devotes the great bulk of its funds to grants-in-aid to the states under the federal-aid highway and federal-aid airport programs.[4]

A similar development is noticeable within the Department of Defense when we compare the older, more traditional activities with the newer types of equipment and weapon systems. For example, the Navy's shipyards, using Navy military and civilian personnel, do three-quarters of the shipbuilding and repair work that the Navy requires. (The one-fourth of the work done by private yards includes nuclear submarines and other exotic equipment.)

In contrast, about nine-tenths of the aircraft and missile production and repair work needed by the Department of Defense is assigned to private aerospace companies. In the case of sophisticated electronics systems, government facilities do less than 3 per cent of the work and the other 97 per cent is contracted out to business firms and nonprofit research institutes in the private sector of the economy. When we get down to scientific instruments, we find that government personnel make only one-fifth of 1 per cent of the amount required by the military establishment.[5]

As a result of these developments, the economic character of federal government spending has shifted sharply. Until World War II and for a few years following the end of the war, wage and salary payments to federal employees continued to be the largest category in the budget. Since then, the biggest item of expenditure has become disbursements under contracts with the private sector for goods and services that business firms and others provide to government agencies. Although smaller in absolute size, the two fastest growing elements in the budget have been grants-in-aid to state and local governments and transfer payments to individuals.

Thus, increasingly, federal functions are being performed in the private sector and by state and local governments via the contract and grant mechanisms. It would seem appropriate to sketch out briefly some of the major implications of the large-scale federal use of these two mechanisms. The more detailed economic impacts will be dealt with in later chapters.

The Growth of the Government-Oriented Corporation

As government agencies, notably those dealing with national security matters, have come to depend on new systems and equipment of a highly scientific content, they have grown to depend less and less on their own laboratories and arsenals to design and produce the material they use. The research, development and production of military, atomic energy, and aerospace products are increasingly being performed in the private sector via government contracts with large industrial corporations.

Were the governmental purchases similar to those of the private sector, this might not be a noteworthy development. However, so much of these procurement funds is devoted to fairly exotic items for which there are rarely established private markets—missiles, space vehicles, nuclear-powered aircraft carriers, desalinization systems, atomic energy items, and so forth. As a result, the companies serving the specialized government market develop capabilities different than those required for successful operation in traditional commercial markets. There is a feedback here. As these companies become less effective in competing for private business and more adept at obtaining public contracts, they become heavily dependent on the government customer. Conversely, agencies such as the Department of Defense and NASA maintain little capability to produce the equipment that they need for many of their missions. Hence, they have come to rely almost entirely on these government-oriented corporations. Both parties—private and public—become "locked-in" to a symbiotic relationship where they depend upon each other.

Here, too, there has been a demonstration effect. Other government agencies that require on occasion large-scale technological development and production efforts also turn to the government-oriented corporations. In most cases to date, these are the same corporations as those which dominate the military market and the products that they produce are quite similar. The two largest examples are space systems for NASA—an outgrowth of military ICBM programs—and the development of a supersonic transport aircraft (SST) under the sponsorship of the Department of Transportation—an extension of military aircraft developments. Thus far, the government-oriented corporations have not played an important role in domestic welfare programs. The growing pressures for changing this situation are covered in Chapters 2 and 3.

Institutional Innovations

Simultaneously with its increasing use of the government-oriented corporation, the federal government has been experimenting with a variety of even newer mechanisms in carrying out its expanding functions. Although regional compacts among a group of states are traditional, one of the more recent innovations is the establishment of intergovernmental commissions encompassing both state and federal governments. In a sense, this grouping represents a response to the oft-voiced criticism that, although subnational units of government are needed in a nation of two hundred million inhabitants, state boundaries have become archaic in terms of modern needs. Chapter 4 examines the activities of these new regional agencies that, in a limited way, promise to remake the political map of the United States.

Another innovation in public-private sector relationships is the growing utilization by the federal government of ostensibly private nonprofit organizations that have been set up specifically to carry out a function which the federal government has stated that it would support. Education and welfare, to date, represent the major uses of this device, which almost completely bypasses states and their localities. The extent to which these new mechanisms are neither wholly private nor wholly public will be explored.

The Massive Use of State and Local Governments

In addition to these newer mechanisms, the federal government has placed increased reliance on working through state and local governments via grants-in-aid. The relative role of the federal government and state-local governments has undergone a major shift during the period since the end of World War II. In 1946, the federal establishment conducted its operation with a civilian work force of about two million; the states and their subdivisions reported total employment at a shade under four million.

At the present time, despite a three-fold increase in the national budget, the federal government still operates with about the same labor force that it did over two decades ago. In contrast, the number of employees of state and local governments more than doubled during the same period, and now exceeds eight million. The tendency for the federal government to be a policy formulator rather than a "doer" does not seem to have been adopted by the states or cities. The one-way flow of financial assistance (from the national government to state and local units) has served to maintain their different characteristics.

Although federal grants-in-aid to the states date back to the earliest part of the nineteenth century, they were quantitatively unimportant prior to the New Deal. In 1929, total federal grants came to about $100 million or 3 per cent of the $3 billion federal budget of that laissez-faire period. By 1941, a ninefold increase had taken place. However, this only resulted in an aid expenditures total of $900 million out of a $19 billion budget. In absolute terms, the vast bulk of the expansion in federal grants to state and local governments has occurred since the end of World War II. Currently, such federal-aid expenditures come to about $20 billion a year, compared to total domestic civilian expenditures by the federal government in the neighborhood of $100 billion. Likewise, the growth in the number and variety of federal assistance programs to states and localities (anti-poverty, library facilities, fisheries, pollution control) has taken place mainly during the past two decades. In the long-term development of the unique form of federalism characterizing governmental institutions in the United States, the rise of the grant-in-aid constitutes a very recent phenomenon.

There is a widespread tendency to think of these grants as gifts and thus to assume that they merely add to the financial resources of the recipients. Such is hardly the case. For the typical grant program, the state—prior to receiving any federal money—must obtain approval of its detailed program and plans from the federal agency overseeing the disbursement of aid funds.

This results in the federal government's not only reviewing the use to which its funds are put by the states but also reviewing the matching funds which the states put up themselves. The cumulative control and influence which the federal departments can exert over their counterpart departments in the states thus becomes substantial. The question arises inevitably as to the extent the grant-in-aid system is converting the states into veritable agents of the federal government. Is there the possibility that the states may become the civilian counterparts to the arsenal-like, government-oriented corporations in the military sphere? The actual extent to which federal control and influence are exercised varies substantially both by program and region, but cumulative effect is quite substantial. Possibilities for significant changes in the relationships between the federal government and states and localities—which are possible developments during the post-Vietnam period—are covered in Chapter 5.

The Growth of the Analytical Staffs

Of the several ways in which the federal government has responded to the challenge of managing its large, varied, and rapidly expanding activities, one of the most important and unnoticed is the development and expansion of its internal organizational capabilities, particularly at staff levels. The increasing size and influence of the analytical and policy staffs within the federal government represents one of the most important and far-reaching developments in the public sector during the past three decades.

The prototype was the Bureau of the Budget, that den of green eyeshade accountants which was set up by the Budget and Accounting Act of 1921 in order to pull together the appropriation requests of the various executive agencies. It may be interesting to note that President Woodrow Wilson originally vetoed the Act, and it was finally passed and signed during the administration of Warren Harding. In any event, the Budget Bureau rested peacefully in the Treasury Department—a haven for old-line agencies—until 1939.

The establishment in 1939 of the Executive Office of the President (EOP) represented a significant event in the development of analytical expertise in the executive branch of the federal government. This occurred in response to the recommendation of the Brownlow Commission, or technically, the President's Committee on Administrative Management. The purpose of setting up the new government unit was to give the President staff assistance for a longer term and on a larger scale than had been available through the short-term political appointees on the White House staff or by informal loans of personnel from the operating departments and agencies.

The Budget Bureau was transferred to the new EOP to serve as a general managerial arm of the President, as well as budgeteer. Several less durable agencies were also moved to the EOP, such as the National Resources Planning Board. However, it was the Budget Bureau which gradually took on the nature of a general staff. The traditional responsibility for preparing the annual budget grew in importance as federal spending rose from $3 billion in 1939 to $41 billion in 1949 and $184 billion estimated for 1969.[6] In addition, the bureau took on legislative clearance and organizational and statistical responsibilities.

The legislative clearance role may be the most powerful and least well-known function of the EOP. When congressional committees consider a bill, it is customary for them to ask the various interested federal agencies for their views. For example, a bill being considered by the House Ways and Means Committee to eliminate the excise tax on gasoline used by farmers would be sent to the Treasury Department for comments (because they collect the tax), to the Agriculture Department (which is concerned with the welfare of farmers), and the Transportation Department (which spend these taxes for the federal-aid highway program). In order to achieve some consistency among the reports that the three agencies would send the Ways and Means Committee, they are required by the President to first submit their proposed reports to the Bureau of the Budget for "clearance." The Bureau's Office of Legislative Reference attempts to achieve a common administration position, often meeting with both agency and White House personnel. The bureau has several alternatives to choose from. It may tell the agency that its proposed report is "in accord with the program of the President." This is the highest form of endorsement, indicating that the agency has the White House's blessing. Frequently, the agency may be told that there is "no objection" to the submission of the proposed report. On occasion, however, the agency may be instructed to revise the report.

After a bill passes both Houses of the Congress and awaits Presidential signature, the bureau gets involved again. Its Office of Legislative Reference then requests the agencies concerned for their views as to whether the bill should be signed or vetoed. Again the bureau's role here is to develop an administration position; this may include drafting the signature or veto message. Clearly, the bureau exercises a pivotal role in the legislative process.

In addition to its budgeting and legislative clearance functions, the Budget Bureau also prepares plans for the President to reorganize government departments and agencies, such as the recent establishment of a new Department of Transportation, by combining agencies formerly located in other departments. The bureau reviews proposed executive orders, approves agency statistical questionnaires before they are sent to the public, and exercises related responsibilities which have accrued to it over the past three decades as the President's principal managerial aid.

Since the end of World War II, several other important units have been created in the Executive Office, although none of them rival the Budget Bureau in the general sweep of their authority and influence. (See Table 1–1.) The Employment Act of 1946, in setting up national goals of maximum employment, production, and purchasing power, also established the Council of Economic Advisers (CEA) in the EOP. In addition to advising the President on the economic outlook and the economic impli-

TABLE 1-1 *The Growth of the Executive Office of the President*

1939 Unit	1939 No. of Employees	1949 Unit	1949 No. of Employees	1959 Unit	1959 No. of Employees	1969 Unit	1969 No. of Employees
The White House	45	The White House	220	The White House	395	The White House	325
Bureau of the Budget	103	Bureau of the Budget	522	Bureau of the Budget	422	Bureau of the Budget	503
National Resources Planning Board	142	National Security Resources Board	283	Office of Civil and Defense Mobilization	1,821*	Office of Emergency Preparedness	240
Office of Government Reports	280	Council of Economic Advisers	39	Council of Economic Advisers	31	Council of Economic Advisers	60
		National Security Council	16	National Security Council	62	National Security Council	34
				Advisory Committee on Governmental Organization	6	National Aeronautics and Space Council	26
						Office of Science and Technology	54
						Office of the Special Representative for Trade Negotiations	28
						National Council on Marine Resources and Engineering Development	22
TOTAL	570	TOTAL	1,080	TOTAL	2,737	TOTAL	1,292

* Includes civil defense activities subsequently transferred to the Department of Defense.
SOURCE: Annual federal budget documents.

cations of proposed government actions, the CEA increasingly has come to develop and monitor economic policies conducted by the operating departments and agencies.

The CEA has served frequently as the President's liaison with the private sector in the case of impending price increases in important industries. The role here is a great deal more than advisory to the President, and begins to approach the nature of an informal ambassador to the heads of large private companies. Indeed, one recent CEA chairman, Gardner Ackley, was subsequently appointed Ambassador to Italy. Frequently, the CEA chairman also heads important interdepartmental committees charged with developing administration policies. Recent examples include the Committee on the Economic Impact of Defense and Disarmament—which dealt primarily with the question of government aid to groups adversely affected by defense cutbacks—and the Cabinet Committee on Price Stability. The latter was instructed to determine what actions could be taken to reduce inflationary pressures.

In a more specialized area, the Office of Science and Technology (OST) has been set up in the EOP to attempt to introduce greater consistency and rationality in the wide gamut of research and development programs conducted by the federal government. The head of OST is also designated as science advisor to the President and attempts to carry out the difficult chore of establishing a national science policy, as well as advising the President on scientific aspects of specific policy questions.

The Office of Emergency Preparedness, also in the EOP, originally was set up to plan for the controlled economy which would accompany or follow a nuclear war. Increasingly, this office has been looked to by the President for liaison work with the state governments in a wide variety of civilian functions. The last several heads of the agency have been former governors and hence have been a natural contact point for state officials concerned with grants-in-aid and other aspects of federal-state relations. One recent head of the agency, a former governor of Florida stated, "it was my privilege to serve as the President's

Ambassador to the States." He pointed out that in one six-month period, he led teams of federal officials to forty state capitals to confer with governors and their staffs on improving grant-in-aid programs.[7]

Other agencies in the EOP include the National Security Council and the National Aeronautics and Space Council; these are more in the nature of high-level interdepartmental committees with small permanent staffs housed in the EOP rather than staff extensions of the White House or the Presidency. The anti-poverty agency, the OEO, is also officially lodged in the EOP, but its functions are more similar to those of the typical large-line agency.

As many of its large operating programs have been designated for transfer to regular departments, data on OEO are not included in Table 1-1. In February 1969, President Richard M. Nixon told the Congress that programs accounting for about one-half of the OEO budget were to be so "spun off." The Head Start program of preschool education, the comprehensive health centers, and the foster grandparent programs will be delegated to the Department of Health, Education, and Welfare. The Job Corps program for disadvantaged youngsters will be transferred to the Department of Labor.

However, the rise of the analytical staffs and their increasingly sophisticated capabilities has not served as a substitute for the tendency of the federal government departments to contract out or delegate program execution. Rather, this development has made possible the increasingly difficult task of coordinating the internal and external activities funded through the public purse.

Several of the largest operating agencies of the federal government have also begun to develop the capabilities of their analytical staffs. The most ambitious efforts to date have been on the part of the two largest departments—Defense and HEW.

The National Security Act of 1947 created a National Military Establishment which was charged with administering three agencies, the departments of Air Force, Army, and Navy. Shortly afterwards, legislation was enacted changing the title of the overseeing agency to the Department of Defense; the Office of the Secretary of Defense (OSD) thus began a decade of rapid development.

At first, the growth of the OSD staffs proceeded along quite conventional paths, covering financial management, logistics, personnel, and other traditional functions. In 1961, a metamorphosis began to occur as the then new Secretary of Defense, Robert S. McNamara, recruited large numbers of systems analysts, weapons evaluators, cost analysts, economists, statisticians, and other products of the think tanks (notably Rand Corporation), the more conventional research institutes, and colleges and universities. These staffs brought with them new ways of examining military programs (the so-called program packages) and new ways of evaluating the expensive weapon systems proposed by each of the services (cost-effectiveness analysis).

The new methodological tools and the people to use them gave the Secretary an unparalleled capability to oversee the wide variety of operations conducted by the departments of Air Force, Army, and Navy, as well as the growing number of separate military activities, such as the Defense Supply Agency and the Defense Intelligence Agency. The program-package approach, in effect, was a substitute for service integration, without the formal loss of face on the part of the services. Previously, military funds were allocated primarily by service, with each service possessing wide latitude to distribute its funds among its various component activities (for example, the funds appropriated to the Navy were allocated among carrier task forces, nuclear submarines, the Marine Corps, and similar items which are in the main not comparable or substitutable).

Under the program-package approach, in contrast, the funds are allocated to several basic establishment-wide functions involving closely related programs (program packages); the services compete against each other for shares of each package. For example, in the competition for funds for the "continental defense" program package, the Army may offer its anti-ICBM program, the Air Force its air defense jet fighter aircraft, and the

Navy its picket ships and coast patrol vessels. How can decisions be made among these and other similar alternative methods of enhancing the defensive posture of the continental United States? By estimating the relative cost-effectiveness of each of the alternatives, via a methodology originated at the Rand Corporation, it can be determined, or at least estimated, which combination of weapons will achieve the military objectives at lowest cost. And who makes this determination? It is no longer a matter for separate choice by each of the services. Because these establishment-wide decisions cut across traditional service lines, the Secretary of Defense and his key subordinates must make them. Hence, the development of staff capability to analyze and evaluate enabled line decision-making and delegation to proceed with greater confidence.

The Pentagon experience has had some "demonstration" effect on other government agencies, but to date on a much more limited extent. For example, HEW—the second largest federal agency in terms of expenditures and the variety of activities—has attempted to follow suit, but on a much smaller scale. The HEW analytical staffs, some of whom were both at Rand Corporation and the Pentagon previously, have been developing tools of economic analysis which can be used to evaluate civilian government programs. Efforts to date comprise mainly benefit-cost studies of human investment programs such as education, training, and health. This approach attempts to help decision-makers to identify those programs for which the benefits exceed the costs to the greatest degree.

Thus far, it does not appear that the analytical efforts in HEW —or similar attempts in the Department of Transportation— have yet exerted an important influence on actual decisions authorizing new government programs or altering support of existing governmental activities. Rather, these early analyses appear to be more in the nature of developmental efforts designed to advance the state-of-the-art, which will become operational at a later date. Although detailed examination of the application of these economic concepts to the allocation of resources in the public sector is deferred to a later chapter, it would appear that in the future benefit-cost and similar analytical techniques will be able to increase the decision-making capability of the heads of civilian government agencies in a manner similar to the cost-effectiveness analysis of the Pentagon.

Policy Questions to Be Faced

The intertwining of the public and private sectors and of federal with state-local activities, although it undoubtedly is useful in carrying on specific functional programs, also raises important long-run questions of public policy. It may be helpful to indicate some of these policy questions as a backdrop for the analysis which is contained in the chapters that follow.

DO WE NEED TO CHANGE THE NATURE OF GOVERNMENT-INDUSTRY BUSINESS RELATIONS? There seems to be some danger of the unintended socialization or nationalization of a branch of private industry via the government contract mechanism. When a company receives most of its business, year in and year out, from one federal agency there may be some tendency for it to act more like a government bureau than a private enterprise. It is useful to explore the nature of these relationships and to determine whether the work for the government can be conducted efficiently without the "arsenalization" of the private contractors.

DO WE NEED TO MODIFY THE PATTERN OF FEDERAL-STATE-LOCAL RELATIONS? The nature of the federal grant-in-aid needs to be examined in some detail. Other methods need to be considered whereby the fiscal strength of the federal government can be drawn upon to finance domestic programs conducted at state or local levels.

DO WE UNDERSTAND THE ECONOMIC IMPACTS OF THE NEW PUBLIC SECTOR? In recent years it has become well known that a large public sector, such as characterizes most advanced nations, has important effects on the national economy. Tools of fiscal policy, such as changes in tax rates and expenditure levels, have been highly developed and, with the advent of the New Economics in Washington, have been widely utilized.

However, there has been a general lack of understanding of the nature of the new, modern public sector, even on the part of economists within the federal government itself. This ignorance, particularly of the intertwined nature of the new "contractual" public sector, has impeded the ability to maintain economic stability during periods of major shifts in the size and composition of the public sector. This shortcoming has been most apparent during the buildup periods of both the Korean and Vietnam wars. Substantial inflation occurred as a result of the expansion of production by defense contractors before government policy-makers were fully aware of the consequences. In both cases, by the time they attempted to act, considerable inflationary pressures had worked their way into the economic system. Analogous problems, on the downside, result when major reductions in military spending accompany the achievement of peace.

The tools of macroeconomic analysis need to be sharpened to deal with the emerging mixed economy, particularly during periods of abrupt shift in the nature and composition of government spending. Chapter 6 shows how the analysis presented here can be used to develop better tools for formulating and executing economic and fiscal policy.

DO WE NEED NEW METHODS OF ALLOCATING PUBLIC RESOURCES? The traditional tools of governmental budgeting were never very good, focusing as they did primarily on details and often trivia. ("Why is the personnel office requesting so many more filing cabinets?" "Does the assistant administrator really need a new car?") This approach may have been tolerable when the Congress and the President were mainly reviewing the number of clerks to be hired and the kinds of desks to be purchased. However, antiquated methods of decision-making cease to be acceptable when public resources to be allocated approach the magnitude of $200 billion a year and involve complex selections among contracting-out to the private sector, joint efforts with state and local governments, and transfer payments to many millions of individuals.

As a result of the McNamara and related reforms, the tools and concepts of governmental budgeting are now being shifted from preoccupation with the expenses of government personnel to the major activities and functions carried on by each of the departments and agencies. Nevertheless, the basic functions of the national government still cut across the various agencies and departments, and the process of allocating public resources from the position of the individual agency or department is still too restricted a viewpoint. Of even greater concern is the tendency to ignore what economists call "distributional" considerations, that is, the extent to which the benefits of government programs are broadly distributed among the population and particularly to the lower-income groups. For example, under benefit-cost analysis as it is currently used to evaluate governmental investment programs, it is not unusual to come across a proposed project which is enthusiastically recommended for approval because the total benefits exceed the total costs; yet virtually all the benefits would be obtained by a single company or other private interest and all of the costs would be borne by the general taxpayer. In describing a proposed project in Indiana, the Secretary of the Army wrote to the Speaker of the House of Representatives, "The benefits from the recommended project modification will accrue entirely from savings in transportation costs on commerce in iron ore unloaded at the dock of a single steel company." In this case, the private beneficiary was required to pay one-half of the cost.[8]

In a more fundamental way, the intimately related questions, "Who gets the benefits?" and "Who pays the costs?" represent the meeting ground of economics and politics in the public sector. However, there is no need to go to the extreme of some economists and dismiss these questions as being amenable to answers in only a subjective or arbitrary fashion. In a sense, they involve the dichotomy between what is sometimes called allocative efficiency and distributional equity. A narrow economic approach would contend that government resources should be invested solely with an eye to their measurable dollar return (the excess of benefits over costs). However, an equally narrow (and perhaps not as fashionable as formerly) noneconomic approach would contend that an individual or group, and their political representatives, should be concerned practically and simply with maximizing the benefits they receive regardless of the cost to the rest of society.

Actually, any balanced approach would steer clear of either of these extremes. We need to be concerned with both increasing the size of the pie (through economic investments of public resources) and more equitably distributing the pie. At the margin, we should be willing to trade off some allocative efficiency for greater distributional equity, and we do so in the real world. The nation is willing to subsidize new businesses set up in ghetto areas—but to a limited extent. Also, we are willing to subsidize large companies involved in the development of our natural resources—but not without limit. This is not an either-or type of situation, but one characterized by compromise and change. In a later chapter, some efforts are made to show how economic analysis can contribute something useful to these twin questions of efficiency of production and distribution of benefits.

The horizon of governmental budgeting needs to be broadened substantially. Resource allocation within the public sector can be accomplished in a more comprehensive and effective manner than is done at present. Some of the more promising alternatives available are examined in Chapter 7.

WHAT SHOULD BE THE FUTURE STRUCTURE OF THE PUBLIC SECTOR? Down to the present time, the two major mechanisms available for decentralizing federal activities—the government-oriented corporation and grants to the states and localities—have been utilized in quite an independent fashion. The government-oriented corporation has been used in national security and related high technology programs, mainly those conducted by the

Defense Department, NASA, the Atomic Energy Commission (AEC), and for the development of the SST. Grants-in-aid have been used primarily in connection with welfare and other domestic programs.

The difference in the quality of resources made available for public programs by the two mechanisms is striking. Compare the income and educational levels of the engineers, scientists, and other highly educated, innovative professionals working on missile or space systems with the typical employee of state highway departments or local welfare agencies. Compare the concentration of science and technology in national security programs with their virtual absence from domestic welfare activities. For example, all state agencies combined (excluding colleges and universities) spent a mere $88 million for research and development in 1965 compared to the federal government's research and development budget of $16.5 billion. Of the latter amount, $14.5 billion was devoted to military applications, space, and atomic energy.[9]

With the growing federal involvement in newer and perhaps even more difficult problem areas, such as easing racial tensions by reducing urban poverty and combating the growing pollution of the physical environment, rising pressures are already being felt for utilizing both mechanisms, grants to states and government-oriented corporations. Increasingly, persons familiar with both developments are suggesting that some of the research and development and other high quality resources now devoted to national defense purposes could usefully be employed to meet pressing domestic needs. In this regard, the states and the large private corporations may either be viewed as alternatives or as possible cooperating mechanisms.

To the extent that the government-oriented corporations compete with the states for federal funds for carrying out activities with a national purpose, the potential may be created for another major shift in our federal system. It would appear that the reliance that federal departments place on state agencies to execute programs does not arise so much from any federal concern over the need to strengthen the states, but from a simple realization of the administrative limitations of the national government. (This latter point is bolstered, of course, by political pressures coming from the states.)

Hence, the private corporations may constitute a growing alternative method of conducting the business of the national government, in civilian as well as military matters. It is conceivable that, in time, a new and added type of federalism could be developed—between the national government and at least some selected segments of private industry. "Corporate" forms of government, of course, have had some unfortunate historical experiences, particularly in Western Europe, but the parallel should not be drawn too tightly. Nevertheless, a major expansion of the role of the government-oriented corporations to domestic programs, particularly at the expense of the states, would be cause for serious public concern.

At this relatively early stage of development, it is possible to discern some promising alternatives. For example, the government-oriented corporations might work directly with state and local governments. Indeed, as shown in Chapters 2 and 3, some are doing this already.

Perhaps the federal government can take specific actions to encourage the science-intensive, government-oriented corporations to work with state and local governments. Such encouragement might be given through federal funds creating new "markets"—at the state and/or local level—for poverty reduction, urban transportation systems, environmental pollution control, and similar activities. Other alternatives may be offered. Some, such as more generous general assistance by the national government to the states, would represent a less sharp break with the status quo; others—the negative income tax being a prominent example—would reduce the need for detailed program activities in the welfare field, whether by federal agencies or delegated organizations in the public or private sectors.

However, the nature of these alternatives needs to be considered far more deeply than has been done to date before adequate public policies can be developed and implemented. Chapter 8 examines the various possibilities for major change in the future structure of the public sector likely to be made in response to the developing program needs of the nation. Finally, some of the more durable underlying trends are identified and analyzed.

NOTES

1. Peter F. Drucker, "The Sickness of Government," *Public Interest,* No. 14 (Winter 1969), p. 17.
2. *Economic Report of the President, January 1969,* (Washington, D.C.: U.S. Government Printing Office, 1969), p. 297.
3. U.S. Bureau of the Budget, *Budget of the United States Government for the Fiscal Year 1968* (Washington, D.C.: U.S. Government Printing Office, 1967), pp. 340–343; Statistical Office of the United Nations, *Statistical Yearbook, 1966* (New York, 1967), pp. 578, 654; U.S. Bureau of the Census, *Compendium of State Government Finances, 1965* (Washington, D.C.: U.S. Government Printing Office, 1967), p. 10, and *Local Government Finances in Selected Metropolitan Areas in 1965–66* (Washington, D.C.: U.S. Government Printing Office, 1968), p. 17.
4. The data in this section were obtained from U.S. Bureau of the Budget, *Object Class Analysis, Budget for Fiscal Year 1969* (Washington, D.C.: March 1968, processed).
5. These data were obtained from Murray L. Weidenbaum, *The Military Space Market: The Intersection of the Public and Private Sectors* (Washington University, Department of Economics, Working Paper 6712, September 1967), pp. 43–44.
6. *Economic Report of the President, January 1969* (Washington, D.C.: U.S. Government Printing Office, 1969), p. 297.
7. Farris Bryant, "Federalism vs. Federalization: The Role of State and Local Governments in a Federal System," in *Creative Federalism and Priorities in Public Programs* (New York: Tax Foundation, Inc., 1968), p. 7.
8. U.S. Congress House, *Great Lakes Harbors Study—Second Interim Report on Indiana Harbor, Indiana,* Doc. No. 227, 89th Cong., 1st Sess. (Washington, D.C.: U.S. Government Printing Office, 1965), p. v.

9. U.S. National Science Foundation, *R & D Activities in State Government Agencies, Fiscal Years 1964 and 1965* (Washington, D.C.: U.S. Government Printing Office, 1967), p. vii, and *Federal Funds for Research Development, and Other Scientific Activities, Fiscal Years 1964, 1965 and 1966* (Washington, D.C.: U.S. Government Printing Office, 1965), XIV, 22–26.

2

THE GOVERNMENT-ORIENTED
CORPORATION

It has become fashionable to assert that, since federal purchases of goods and services amount to only one-tenth of our gross national product, they can have only a marginal impact on the national economy. But, such a simpleminded aggregate comparison ignores the fundamental long-term influences that these purchases are exerting on the structure of the private sector of the economy and on the relationship between the public and private sectors.

The impact on private industry of large-scale government contracts of a high-technology nature has been striking. In the past, the industries with which the federal government dealt in securing the bulk of its equipment were primarily the traditional large manufacturers for the civilian economy—the automotive, machinery, shipbuilding, steel, and oil industries—which relied on the government for only a small portion of their sales and profits.

In the current scientific age, the older industries have declined in prominence in the government market and newer research and development-oriented industries have come to the fore—those dealing in aircraft, missiles, electronics, and scientific instruments. There are significant differences between these newer industries and more conventional ones. The most striking difference is the reliance of the newer industries almost entirely on government sales for their business.

There is another side to the coin. As Don Price, a leading analyst of the cross relations between government and science, points out, the system of contracting with industry has given the military great advantages of flexibility and has enabled them to make use of managerial talents that cannot be found in adequate quantity within the government.[1] However, the government-industry relationship that has evolved in the conduct of these high-technology public programs is a novel one. As will be shown, the relationship is far from the arm's-length transaction associated with either the commercial market or with sealed bidding for government civilian contracts. Rather the relationship moves from that of private seller dealing with public buyer to government agent serving a government department.

The following analysis of these government-oriented corporations tends to demonstrate that the long-term dealings between the federal government and the major companies serving high technology government markets are changing the nature of both the public sector of the American economy and a large branch of American industry.[2] The close connections between the government and its contractors have been viewed in various ways, some favorable and others quite unfavorable. Andrew Shonfield, for example, views this form of government-industry relationship as an important step toward rational economic planning.[3] Others have noted the same phenomenon with fear or opposition. Walter Adams, contending that the award of the bulk of defense contracts is "as much the result of political as economic bargaining," describes a conversion process whereby the private contractor has been transformed into a "quasi-governmental, mercantilist operation, maintained in a privileged position by 'royal' franchise."[4]

This study expresses a somewhat different concern. In a sense, the close continuing relationship between such government agencies as the Department of Defense and their major suppliers is resulting in a convergence between them, blurring and reducing much of the distinction between public and private activities in an important branch of the American economy. In turn, this evolving government-industry relationship is raising important questions of public policy. To what extent are the government-oriented corporations public rather than private mechanisms? As we will see, many of the assets they use are owned by the government and much of what they produce as well as important aspects of their internal operations are determined by the government. Conversely, to what extent are these corporations, which at least ostensibly are lodged in the private sector, carrying out functions which can or should be conducted by regular government agencies? To some degree, the production of weapons by these government contractors is a substitute for the operation of government arsenals. Perhaps it is no longer appropriate to use the relatively simple concepts of government regulation of industry or of government competition with business, which were developed to deal with less complex situations. In some ways, the newer relationship can be viewed as a partnership whereby both the public and private sectors work together in achieving important national purposes unattainable via separate efforts in either sector of the economy. This approach would call for greater cooperation between the public and private organizations and for some reductions in adversary relationships between the two.

Yet another viewpoint holds that one of the partners is more senior than the other. Hence, a growing concern is evident with the possibilities for private corporations assuming, in practice, important government functions. These may range from policy-making to program execution. The public policy response to this concern would be quite different—to reduce the role of private industry in the conduct of the government's business or, at least, to more carefully circumscribe the use of the contract device in carrying out federal programs.

A related possibility has not received as much public attention: the extent to which these government agents are losing some

of the private characteristics and are becoming virtual append-
ages of the government. Although the available evidence is
hardly one-sided, much of it indicates that there is cause for
some concern on this latter score. In some ways, the federal
government is taking on the traditional role of the private en-
trepreneur while the companies are behaving less like other
corporations and more like government agencies or arsenals.

How can we maintain the independence and entrepreneurial
abilities of the private companies that do most of their business
with the government while preserving the vital interest of the
federal government (that is, in both the quality of government
programs and in their costs to the Treasury)?

A word of caution is in order. The tendency for a convergence
between national security agencies and their contractors that
we shall be discussing in this chapter is not meant to evoke the
conspiratorial flavor of so much of the discussions of a so-called
military-industrial complex. Nor does it lend support to the much
broader contention of John Kenneth Galbraith that the large
modern corporation is becoming part of the governmental administrative complex. Professor Galbraith contends, in his *New
Industrial State*, that "the mature corporation, as it develops,
becomes part of the larger administrative complex associated
with the state. In time the line between the two will disappear."[5]

To the contrary, an attempt is made to demonstrate that the
convergence phenomenon described is limited to one branch of
American industry—essentially the large military and space systems contractors. In fact, it will be shown that the government-
oriented corporation is becoming measurably different from large
American business firms that primarily cater to industrial and
consumer markets. Also, the following analysis does not reveal
the superior efficiency of these corporations, which is supposed
to be a characteristic of the "new industrial state." In a sense,
the following analysis stands much of the preceding argument
on the military-industrial complex and government-industry relationship on its head. The concern in most of the previous writ-

ings is on the alleged deleterious effects on the government and on society resulting from the expanded role of private industry. In contrast, much of the attention here is focused on the adverse effects on private industry of governmental involvement and regulations, notably on the science-based enterprises that look to the federal government for their basic markets.

In a sense, the analytical basis underlying this approach and that of Galbraith is similar. Both attempt to generalize from the relationship between the military establishment and the large defense contractors. Galbraith cites General Dynamics Corporation, North American Aviation, Boeing, Raytheon, and Lockheed Aircraft Corporation as the prototypes of the "new industrial state." As we will see, these organizations are hardly representative of American industry as a whole.[6] Moreover, the relationships between the federal government and the commercially oriented companies (for example, United States Steel, Continental Can, General Foods, Firestone Tire and Rubber Corp., Anheuser-Busch) are closer to that of adversary or regulator than patron-benefactor or close associate.

We need to begin by examining the evolving role of the government-oriented corporation. This role can be explained in good measure by the changing nature of government purchases from the private sector and the rather atypical method of competing for this government business.

In recent years the federal government has become by far the largest single buyer in the American economy. When a count was last made, it was purchasing over three and a half million different items.[7] About $60 billion of purchases from business firms are now made yearly, compared to only $8 billion as recently as 1950.[8] Simultaneously, two basic changes have occurred which are of more fundamental importance than the increase in volume alone. These developments involve the types of items which the government buys and the method of procurement which it uses.

Federal purchases of goods and services are no longer characterized by a situation whereby a great number of firms present sealed bids offering to sell fairly standard commercial stock items. If this were still the case, it is most unlikely that the phenomenon of the government-oriented corporation would have arisen at all. Instead, the bulk of the purchases consist of specialized commodities, typically highly engineered systems designed and produced to the government's own specifications and for which there are no established private markets—missiles, space vehicles, nuclear-powered carriers, desalinization systems, and atomic energy items. Table 2–1 shows the estimated distribution of federal purchases in 1969.

TABLE 2–1 *Federal Contracts Awarded to the Private Sector. Fiscal Year 1969 Estimate (Percentage Distribution)*

Agency	Per Cent
Department of Defense-Military Functions	73
Department of Agriculture	5
National Aeronautics and Space Administration	4
Atomic Energy Commission	3
General Services Administration	2
Post Office	2
Department of Health, Education, and Welfare	1
Department of Transportation	1
All others	9
TOTAL	100

SOURCE: U.S. Bureau of the Budget, *Object Class Analysis, Budget for Fiscal Year 1969* (Washington, D.C., March 1968).

The dominance of military and related high-technology procurement is striking. Contract awards by the Department of Defense are three times as large as the grand total for all civilian agencies. Moreover, the purchases of the civilian agencies with the largest totals—nuclear reactors and products for the AEC and aerospace systems for the NASA—bear a closer resemblance to the military than to the civilian agencies. This similarity also covers methods of contracting with the private sector.

The Leading Government Contractors[9]

An analysis of the composition of the firms supplying these government markets lends important insights into the nature of the government-oriented corporations. Because these high-technology markets are so completely subject to the changing needs of the governmental customer, relationships between buyers and sellers differ from those typical in the commercial sector of the economy. By the selection of contractors, the government can control entry and exit, can greatly affect the growth of the firms involved, and can impose its ways of doing business on the companies participating.

The bulk of the contracts are let as a result of negotiation with a group of suppliers chosen by the buyers. The governmental purchasing officials normally request proposals from the firms that they consider to be in a position to undertake the magnitude of research and development and production required. However keen the competition among the prospective suppliers may become, it will relate primarily to their technological capability and not simply to price. Moreover, the intensity of the buyers' demand is far less a direct function of their budgets than of the alternative weapon systems made available through technological advance. When technology produces an ICBM, for example, the federal government suddenly develops a craving for intercontinental missiles.

Major portions of the work contracted for are performed by corporations oriented to public requirements rather than market demands. These government-oriented corporations are companies, or fairly autonomous divisions of large, diversified corporations, whose dominant customers are the defense and space agencies of the federal government. The close, continuing relationship between the government and these corporations is more than regulation by federal agencies or selling in markets where the government is a major determinant of price, as in the case of public utilities, agriculture, or mining. Rather, it is the intertwining of the public and private sectors so that it is difficult to identify when specific entrepreneurial or management functions in a given company are being performed primarily by government agents or by private individuals on business payrolls. As will be described subsequently, the contract mechanism provides the basic means for such governmental intervention.

A relatively limited number of companies receive the bulk of the defense and space contract awards. Over the past decade, the one hundred companies obtaining the largest dollar volume of military prime contracts have accounted for about two-thirds of the Department of Defense total. In the case of NASA, the top one hundred companies currently receive nine-tenths of the total contracts awarded each year.[10]

The focus here is on military and space contracts simply because the data are readily available and the Department of Defense and NASA account for the vast bulk of the purchases that the federal government makes from the private sector. An added justification is that the correspondence between the major Department of Defense and NASA contractors is quite high. For example, 16 of the top 25 NASA suppliers in fiscal 1966 were also among the top 25 Defense Department contractors; the other 9 all made the top one hundred defense list for the year. Moreover, the embryonic market for systems work for other public agencies tends to be dominated by the same companies.

Who are the government-oriented corporations? An analysis of the size distribution of the top one hundred Defense Department contractors provides another dimension to the structure of government markets. The giants of American industry do not dominate, contrary to much of the writing on the so-called military-industrial complex. Rather, the medium-sized corporations receive the largest share of the orders for these high-technology government products. The 27 corporations with assets of $1 billion or over received only 25 per cent of the defense contracts going to the top one hundred in 1965. This group includes General Motors, Ford, Standard Oil of New Jersey, Radio Corporation of America, Uniroyal, Eastman Kodak, Firestone Tire and Rubber Corp., and International Harvester. In contrast, the 30 companies with assets in the $250–$999 million range received 58 per cent of the contracts, the largest share of any group. Typical firms in this category are the aerospace and electronics manufacturers—Boeing, Hughes Aircraft, Lockheed Aircraft Corporation, and North American Aviation. These certainly are not pygmies among business firms in the United States; neither are they at the very top rung of American industry. As might be expected, relatively small companies did proportionally poorer; the 37 companies with assets below $250 million accounted for only 17 per cent of the defense contracts going to the one hundred major defense contractors.

Another dimension of the structure of this government market relates to the extent of dependence on government work among the major contractors, that is, to the nature of the government-oriented corporations. Again, the data indicate that the firms most heavily dependent on military orders—those primarily oriented to government rather than private markets—are the medium-sized companies rather than the giants of the American industry. Of the top one hundred defense contractors in 1965, for the 7 with assets of $5 billion or over, defense contracts equalled less than 10 per cent of their sales in all cases. For those 20 firms with assets in the $1–$5 billion range, defense orders equalled less than 25 per cent of sales.

Also, the majority of the smaller firms, those with assets under $100 million, received defense contracts exceeding 50 per cent of their sales. This experience is hardly typical of the thousands of smaller businesses participating in government markets. Rather, it reflects the nature of the sample, which is limited to firms receiving the largest absolute amounts of defense contracts.

In contrast, 21 out of the 44 firms with assets of $100–$999 million obtained defense contracts exceeding 25 per cent of their sales; in the case of 10 of these firms—AVCO, Collins Radio, General Dynamics Corporation, LTV, Inc., Lockheed Corporation, Martin-Marietta, McDonnell Corporation, Newport News

Shipbuilding, Northrop, and Raytheon—these government orders exceeded half of their sales volume. These are clearly the "government-oriented corporations."

These government-oriented corporations also show a strong tendency to become "conglomerates" within the government markets for high-technology systems, penetrating a wide variety of product areas. For example, the General Dynamics Corporation, a leading producer of military aircraft and missiles, is the number one supplier of nuclear submarines; it is also an important factor in military electronics.

North American Rockwell, another large aircraft and space systems contractor, has become one of the leading companies in military electronics and propulsion systems. Lockheed Aircraft Corporation, in addition to its dominant position in aircraft and missiles, builds ships for the Navy and electronics and propulsion systems for the Army and Air Force.

Not infrequently one of these companies competes against the others for the prime contract for a new weapon system and, simultaneously, its electronics division teams up with one of its competitors and its propulsion division with another. Thus, to cite a general but reasonable example, North American Rockwell might find that it lost a new missile contract to Lockheed but that its Rocketdyne division has been chosen by Lockheed to build the propulsion system of the missile and that General Dynamics Corporation's Stromberg-Carlson division has been assigned the responsibility for the communication system. Thus, the subcontracting may not necessarily broaden the competitive base, but be used to "share the wealth" among the members of the club. This phenomenon, it should be acknowledged, does not arise from any conspiratorial efforts on the parts of these companies. Rather, it reflects their detailed knowledge of each other's capabilities (often through movement of personnel back and forth among the leading military contractors) and the orientation of these companies to serving the requirements of the military customer.

The Nature of Competition

During the past decade, over 80 per cent of the government procurement of military and space products and systems has been made through negotiated rather than sealed-bid purchasing. Clearly, the prices that the government pays for these goods and services are not determined by the interplay of relatively impersonal market forces. Some observers view this situation with concern and relate the lack of impersonal competition and sealed bidding to the concentration of government business within a relatively few firms.

However, the government agencies involved maintain that buying through negotiation with a select number of companies does not signify lack of competition. The Army's Deputy Chief of Staff for Logistics has stated, "The fact is that the great majority of negotiated procurements are made on a highly competitive basis."[11] He cited a case where 189 potential producers of a piece of equipment were solicited and keen price competition ensued. In his comprehensive analysis of the defense market, Professor W. L. Baldwin states, "Comments of Department of Defense officials, industry executives, the trade press, and knowledgeable critics indicate an overwhelming, perhaps unanimous agreement, that competition in the sense of interfirm rivalry is intense in the defense market."[12]

The Armed Services Procurement Act, under which both the Defense Department and NASA operate, requires that awards be made to the bidder whose bid, price and other factors considered, is most advantageous to the government.[13] In practice, there is a variety of other factors on which rival potential suppliers compete. The previous performance of the company may be an extremely useful indicator of its effectiveness on a future contract. The present availability of skilled manpower and other resources also may be an important determinant of its future performance.

The emphasis on noncost factors, particularly in awarding

contracts to develop new systems of a complex nature, has been pointed out on numerous occasions. A director of procurement of the Air Research and Development Command stated to a congressional committee that, in contracting for research, "The most compelling factor is the technical competence of the individual or firm under consideration. . . ."[14]

Some economists prefer to use the term "rivalry" in place of competition in discussing these markets. Usually when an economist uses the term "competition," he means rivalry with price as the weapon. Almost invariably in military, space, and related government contracting, competition means rivalry between potential contractors about any variable but, as we have seen, most often about technical performance. Whether from the buyer's viewpoint competition or rivalry characterizes the military market, from the seller's viewpoint prices are "administered" in the very basic sense of the word.

Measuring Competition

It is helpful to measure the degree of competition or rivalry in these government markets. Using aggregate data, the Department of Defense categorized 50 per cent of its procurements in the fiscal year 1966 as competitive (although their concept of competition more closely approximates the economist's notion of rivalry between two or more competitors). NASA reported that 70 per cent of the value of the contracts that it awarded in the year were competitively let.[15]

Such statistics have been criticized on several occasions. Recently, the Comptroller General chided the Department of Defense for classifying as competitive all awards under $2,500 and contracts for which only one bid was received, although requests for proposals had been sent out to several firms.[16] Unfortunately, comprehensive statistics on individual competitions, including information on the number of companies that actually responded with bids, are not available.

Turnover among Government Suppliers

One method of indirectly analyzing the degree of competition is to examine the turnover among the dominant firms in a given market area. Viewed in isolation, the entrenchment of the dominant firms appears to be striking: 21 of the top 25 contractors in 1966 were also in the top 25 in 1957. These 21 firms included the aerospace leaders, such as Boeing, Lockheed Aircraft Corporation, North American Aviation, General Dynamics Corporation, and United Aircraft. In another sense, of course, these are the companies that are "locked-in" to government business.

It is interesting to compare this result with the turnover during the same period among large American industrial corporations generally. It turns out that exactly 21 of the top 25 industrial firms in 1966, ranked by dollar-sales volume, also were on the list of the top 25 in 1957. The exact correspondence to the defense situation may be quite coincidental. However, the comparison indicates that market concentration is not unique to government purchasing.

The relatively great stability of the dominant firms in the military market, which are mainly the large aerospace and electronics companies, results in good measure from the substantial barriers to both entry into and exit from the specific sub-market for major weapon systems. The entry barriers mainly take the form of scientific development capabilities required to design and produce modern weapon systems. The exit barriers, in contrast, can be inferred from the many unsuccessful attempts these companies have experienced in penetrating commercial markets, as will be described.

In contrast, considerable mobility is evidenced in the ranking of the firms which have large, but not so marked, shares of defense business. Of the next seventy-five firms, 42, or 56 per cent, were not on the list of the top one hundred defense contractors in 1957. Between 1966 and 1967 alone, 25 per cent of the firms on the top one hundred list were replaced. This shift, which occurred primarily among non-aerospace firms, also reflects the changing product mix of government procurement and, hence, the influence of technology. A decade ago, the large missile programs brought many firms into the military market as suppliers of mechanical ground support equipment, fabricators of silos, and builders of tracking stations. The decline in missile procurement and the rise of ordnance required a different set of technical capabilities and a new variety of industries.

Concentration Ratios in Government Markets

Another indirect method of estimating the degree of competition in government or other markets is to examine the degree of concentration of sellers in the major product categories. Such statistics do not reveal the number of competitors or the severity of competition for individual contracts. At the least, however, the data do indicate whether a few or many firms are active in a given market area.

To compute a concentration ratio, it is necessary to rank firms in order of size, starting from the largest in the industry. Then, starting from the top of the list, the percentages of the industry's or market's sales are cumulated usually for the largest four and largest eight. The concentration ratio for a monopoly would, of course, be 100 per cent. The ratio for the largest four firms in a competitive industry would be relatively small, perhaps 5 or 10 per cent. The highly concentrated (oligopolistic) markets would show concentration ratios somewhere in between these two extremes.

Table 2–2 is an attempt to develop concentration ratios for the major segments of the military market. It is based on the unclassified military contract awards reported and categorized by Frost and Sullivan, Inc., in their widely utilized Defense Market Measures System. Product categories for which total contracts awarded in the fiscal year 1967 were under $200 million were eliminated as being too small for meaningful measures of degrees of competition.

It can be seen that the implicit degree of competition varies substantially among the major product categories. Four firms account for 100 per cent of military satellite contracts (by value), but for only 25 per cent of heavy artillery orders. The level of product aggregation used here is based entirely on the limited data that are available.

In order to analyze the data properly, some standards for measuring concentration are necessary. Professors Carl Kaysen and Donald Turner have suggested that high-seller concentration (oligopoly) occurs when the largest eight firms make 33 per cent or more of the sales of an industry. They group oligopolies into two categories. Type I, heavily concentrated industries, exist where the largest eight firms make at least half of the industry's sales. In Type II oligopolies, moderately concentrated industries; the first eight firms make a third or more of the shipments, but less than half.[17]

For 25 out of the 27 major product categories shown in Table 2–2, eight companies account for 50 per cent or more of the market. (These are the highly concentrated markets characterized by Type I oligopolies.) In the other two market categories, eight firms receive a third or more of the contracts (category II oligopolies). By the Kaysen-Turner standards, hence, the military market is estimated to be relatively concentrated. A more stringent definition of oligopolistic market structures has been developed by Joe Bain. Professor Bain suggests that high-seller concentration occurs when the largest eight firms control 70 per cent or more of the sales of an industry.[18] Under the Bain criterion, 22 out of the 27 military market categories show up as highly concentrated, still a strikingly high proportion.

There has been considerable discussion in the literature concerning the validity and usefulness of concentration ratios as measures of industrial concentration and competition. Morris Adelman states that "the concentration ratio is a fairly crude approximation but, so far, it is the only thing we have which fits the requirements of economic theory that it have some relevance to market behavior." Professor Adelman concludes that "as a general statistical matter, the greater the concentration the lower the odds in favor of competitive behavior." He points out that more refined measures have been proposed, but they have not yet proved useful.[19]

More comprehensive data on government markets, and over longer time periods, are needed to provide greater confidence in the conclusions we have reached on the extent of competition. Yet it appears, from the available data, that government procurement tends to be more highly concentrated than American industries as a whole. The markets for major weapon systems may well be characterized as competition among the few.

Public Assumption of Private Decision-Making

The tendency for the military establishment to rely on a fairly limited group of suppliers for the bulk of its needs has resulted in a unique government-industry relationship. In long-term dealings with these corporations that cater primarily to their markets, federal government agencies such as the Department of Defense and NASA gradually have taken over directly or indirectly many of the decision-making functions which are normally the prerogatives of business management. These government procurements are characterized by price and profit redetermination after the sale, unilaterally, on the part of the government via audit and renegotiation.

A detailed analysis of the largest segment of these government markets, Air Force procurement, recently concluded that "a new structural relationship has been created in which the Air Force, as a buyer, makes specific management decisions about policy and detailed procedures within aerospace companies that sell defense systems to the Air Force."[20] This development may well be the most significant long-term impact of governmental procurement expenditures on the private sector of the American economy. Although the present analysis focuses on the impact on industry of the close governmental relationship, similar effects have been reported in academia. In a paper to the National Academy of Sciences, George Pake, the Executive Vice-Chancellor of Wash-

TABLE 2–2 *Concentration Ratios in the Military Market*

Category	Contracts Awarded in Fiscal Year 1967 (millions)	Per Cent of Contracts		
		Top 4 Firms	Top 8 Firms	Top 20 Firms
Surveillance and detection satellites	$ 236	100	100	100
Nuclear submarines	211	99	99	100
Space boosters	263	97	100	100
Fighter aircraft	2,164	97	100	100
Attack aircraft	570	97	100	100
Missile inertial guidance systems	539	97	99	100
Inertial navigation systems	201	96	99	100
Missile reentry vehicles	278	95	99	100
Aircraft fire control systems	414	95	98	99
Transport and tanker aircraft	1,003	94	99	100
Helicopters	1,208	93	99	100
Jet aircraft engines	1,892	93	99	100
Data processing systems	336	83	93	99
Missile solid rocket propulsion systems	356	81	90	96
Combat vehicles	256	74	91	95
Ships and parts	1,391	67	78	88
Surface based sonar systems	278	63	82	97
Countermeasures systems	209	63	76	92
Surface radar systems	215	62	81	96
Missile systems	2,119	59	82	98
Drones	224	59	72	85
Communications systems	224	56	81	95
Navy power systems	887	50	59	72
Administrative and management services	1,458	37	65	95
Artillery fuse systems	497	35	51	79
Aircraft ground handling and service systems	287	25	40	61
Heavy artillery	1,255	25	38	62

SOURCE: Computed from data supplied by Frost and Sullivan, Inc., *Defense Market Measures System,* Fiscal Year 1967.

ington University, stated that university business offices "have been wholly taken over, in effect by Federal procedures, regulations, and auditors." Professor Pake noted that "perhaps the most serious effect of all these red tape problems is a kind of an intangible change in the nature and quality of the university."[21]

The public assumption of, or active participation in, private business decision-making takes three major forms: influencing the choice of products the firm produces, the source of capital funds that it uses, and its internal operations. It needs to be kept in mind, of course, that this government involvement in private industry arises mainly in the case of the government-oriented corporation which operates primarily in the unique and large-scale nature of military weapon system, space system, atomic energy development, and related high-technology purchasing by the government. It hardly characterizes the procurement of standard conventional items by many civilian government agencies through fixed-price contracts awarded via sealed-bid competition.

By awarding massive contracts for research and development (in the order of $10 billion a year) the Department of Defense and NASA have come to strongly influence or determine which new products their essentially common group of contractors will design and produce. The governmental customers thus directly finance the research and development efforts and assume much of the risks for success or failure. In the commercial economy, in contrast, research and development costs normally are recovered only to the extent that they result in the sale of profitable products. Hence, the decisions to embark upon a product research and development program are made by the sellers, who bear the risk of not recovering their technological investment. Of course, government contractors may and do sponsor and fund some of their own research and development effort.

However, the bulk of their research and development is performed under government contract. Over 90 per cent of the aerospace industry's research and development is so funded.[22] Much if not most of the remainder is charged as allowable overhead on their government contracts, having met the approval of contract administration officials. In good measure, military and space product design and development is not produced as an intermediate good but as an end product which the contractor produces for sale to the government under contract awarded before the research and development is undertaken.

A committee of senior government officials, chaired by the then Budget Bureau director David Bell, reported to the President that "the major initiative and responsibility for promoting and financing research and development have in many important areas been shifted from private enterprise (including academic as well as business institutions) to the Federal Government."

The Bell Committee went on to point out that, unlike the present situation where the federal government finances the bulk of the national expenditure for research and development, most of the nation's research achievements prior to World War II occurred with little federal support.[23]

The government also uses its vast financial resources to supply the bulk of the plant and equipment used by its major contractors and also a major part of the working capital that they require. A survey by the Stanford Research Institute of thirteen of the largest military contractors, covering the years 1957 to 1961, revealed that the cost of government-supplied property exceeded gross company property reported on corporate balance sheets ($1,539,000 to $1,463,000).[24] Moreover, much of the company-owned property was used by the commercially oriented divisions of these companies, rather than by the divisions working on government contracts.

During the middle 1960's, strong efforts were made to sell government facilities to private contractors. Many government-oriented corporations launched substantial capital expansion programs of their own. During the Vietnam War, Department of Defense expenditures for additional plant and equipment to be supplied to its contractors have risen sharply, from $56 million in the fiscal year 1965 to an estimated $330 million in the fiscal year 1967.[25] Historically, the major expansions in government-supplied facilities have occurred during wartime periods. Postwar reductions in such assistance have not been on a scale to offset the expansion during hot war. Hence, the long-term trend has been for large-scale federal supply of fixed capital to these governmentally oriented corporations.

In addition, approximately $8 billion of outstanding "progress" payments are held by military contractors.[26] Some firms report that such part payments made by the government to supply working capital to contractors during the long production period on weapon systems exceed their total net worth. Moreover, military procurements regulations provide specific incentives against the use of private working capital. Thus, according to the Armed Services Procurement Regulation (ASPR), progress payments equal to 80 per cent of the costs incurred in government contracts are generally provided without interest charge to the contractors.[27] But, should these companies decide to rely on private sources for working capital, their interest payments may not be charged to the contract and hence must come out of their profits.[28] Presumably, this arrangement results in a smaller total cost for the government because of the lower interest rates paid by the United States Treasury on the funds that it borrows. However, it also increases the extent to which public rather than private capital finances the operations of government contractors. Hence, the financial stake that the government has in the performance of its contractors is increased further.

Perhaps the most pervasive way in which the federal government assumes the management decision-making functions of its systems-type contractors is through the procurement legislation and regulations governing the awarding of these contracts. For example, the ASPR (which comprises over 1600 pages of text and 800 pages of appendices) requires military suppliers to accept on a "take it or leave it" basis many standard clauses in government contracts which give the military contracting and surveillance officers numerous powers over the internal operations of contracting companies. (The same rules tend to apply to NASA since it is also governed by the Armed Services Procurement Act and attempts to follow the ASPR.)[29] These unilaterally determined grants of authority vary from matters of substance to items so minor that they border on the ludicrous. Of course, in many instances these restrictions have been imposed to prevent specific abuses or even to aid the contractors. One extremely knowledgeable defense official, Graeme C. Bannerman, Assistant Secretary of the Navy (Installations and Logistics), stated that these policy and procedural changes "are designed not to provide rigidity or to inhibit judgment but rather to establish a framework within which the widest discretion may be exercised in dealing with each individual transaction."[30]

But then, as Professors George Steiner and William Ryan, commenting on the Bannerman statement, pointed out: "It is difficult for us to see how increasing the number of directives which apply to industry, then placing these detailed regulations in the hands of the average contract administrator, will increase the contractor's freedom."[31]

Certainly, governmental policy-makers rarely consider the cumulative and long-term impacts on company initiative and entrepreneurship. Viewed as a whole, these restrictions represent a new form of government regulation of industry, one that is accomplished not through the traditional independent regulatory commission, subject to the Administrative Procedures Act and similar judicial legislation, but rather through the unilateral exercise of the government's monopsonistic (single buyer) market power.

The governmental "customer" enjoys the power to review and veto company decisions concerning which activities to perform in-house and which to subcontract, which firms to use as subcontractors, which products to buy domestically rather than import, what internal financial reporting systems to establish, what type of industrial engineering and planning system to utilize, what minimum as well as average wage rates to pay, how much overtime work to authorize, and so forth.[32] Or, as Professor

Michael Reagan has put it, "When a business firm enters into a contract with the government . . . the quasi-public nature of the contracting firm is given implicit recognition by requirements that the firm conduct itself similarly to a government agency in abiding by policies that bind such an agency."[33]

My favorite example of the more minor matters covered in the detailed and voluminous military procurement regulations is the prescription that the safety rules followed in the offices and factories of the contractors must be consistent with the latest edition of the Corps of Engineers' safety manual.[34]

This entire philosophy and attitude of close government review of the internal operations of its contractors is so deeply imbedded that when statements such as the following one are added to the ASPR, they evoke no public or industry reaction: "Although the Government does not expect to participate in every management decision, it may reserve the right to review the contractor's management efforts . . ."[35]

Cost-plus contracting has shifted much of the risk-bearing from the industrial seller to the governmental buyer. The use of fixed-price contracts by the Department of Defense has increased in recent years. However, a major share of military contracts still is on a cost-reimbursement basis. As long as this remains the case, the government determines which items of cost are "allowable" as charges to the contract. Hence, to a large extent this determines or at least strongly influences which activities and which items of expenditure the company can profitably undertake (for disallowed costs directly reduce company net profits).

The most important unallowable costs according to the Stanford Research Institute survey of the major defense companies were interest expense, advertising and selling, research and development, and management bonuses. Of course, the government-industry relationship is a dynamic one and numerous changes are made in military procurement regulations in the course of a year. Many of these changes further extend the role of the government in the internal operations of the contractors. Serious efforts were made in the early 1960's to reduce the extent of the close governmental surveillance. However, the more recent tendency has been for increased controls over government contractors. Here is just a sample of new regulations during the year and a half ending October 1967.[36]

In contracts for aircraft tires, tubes, and recapping, the contractor must purchase an amount of rubber from the government's stockpile equal to at least 50 per cent of the value of the contract. The contractor does not actually have to use the rubber from the stockpile in filling the government contract, but can keep it for his commercial work. Similar requirements, although somewhat less restrictive, must be met by contractors who provide aluminum products, while military contractors must buy all of their jewel bearings from the government-owned Turtle Mountain Bearing Plant at Rolla, North Dakota. Of course, if such tie-in contracts were made between two private firms, they would run afoul of the antitrust laws.

In deciding whether the costs of professional and consulting services used by a contractor are an allowable charge to a military contract, the government now decides "whether the services can be performed more economically by employment rather than by contracting"—that is, whether one of its contractors should hire an outside consultant rather than a permanent employee. (The government also assumes the authority to review the qualifications of the consultant.)

Help-wanted advertising is no longer an allowable cost if it is in color. Advertising for employees, if it is to be an allowable cost, must be authorized in advance.

Moreover, the Pentagon recently has reported that it is reviewing "what actions on the part of the government are necessary to assure that compensation paid to contractor employees performing on government contracts is reasonable."[37] Clearly, the trend for increased governmental involvement in private business decision-making is a long-continuing one.

Also, congressional committees have shown a growing concern

during the past year with the efficiency of defense procurement, the profitability of defense contracts, and the controls exercised over federal equipment used by government contractors. The resultant congressional hearings often result in pressures for increasing rather than decreasing government surveillance of its industrial contractors.

Some Long-Term Impacts on the Private Sector

This close, continuing relationship of the major, specialized government contractors to the governmental establishment is producing long-term structural changes on the defense segment of private industry. From the viewpoint of the individual defense-industry executive, Steiner and Ryan reported that when company managers are faced with a large mass of government regulations, they spend time completing forms that might better be devoted to actual management. The typical application of government regulations is designed to insure, on the average, satisfactory performance or, conversely, to prevent failures. However, in doing this, the government often inhibits the performance and innovation on the part of project managers. "Tightened controls resulted in their performing under their capability."[38]

Looking at defense companies as a whole, there are numerous specific indications that these government-oriented corporations have displayed little entrepreneurial initiative. Thus, the well-known dependence of the shipbuilding companies on government contracts and subsidies has contributed to the industry's failure to undertake new product development on its own or otherwise effectively to compete in the open world market. Similarly, the aerospace industry generally has made numerous but mainly only halfhearted efforts to utilize its much vaunted engineering and systems analysis capability to penetrate commercial markets.

Indeed, an examination of the defense industry's largely unsuccessful commercial diversification efforts (see Chapter 3) helps to explain the locked-in or "captive" nature of the government-oriented corporation.

An Analysis of the Governmental Relation

The long-term impacts of the governmental relationship on the private contractors can be examined objectively by comparing statistically the financial results reported by the major government-oriented corporations with those of other large industrial corporations in the United States. The contrasts are quite revealing.

The following six companies were selected because their contracts from the Department of Defense and the NASA were estimated to be more than three-quarters of their total sales volume in 1965, the most recent year for which the data have not been obscured by the special purchasing patterns of the Vietnam War: North American Aviation, Lockheed Aircraft Corporation, General Dynamics Corporation, McDonnell Corporation, Grumman Aircraft Engineering Corporation, and Thiokol Chemical Corporation. These six companies constitute about as many examples of the government-oriented corporation as there are available. A few, notably Hughes Aircraft Company, are privately owned and do not release pertinent information on their operations. For many other large defense contractors, we lack the necessary data because the organizations are subsidiaries or divisions of corporate conglomerates that only release financial information on the total company (for example, Martin-Marietta, Litton Industries, and Textron).

A six-company civilian-oriented sample was chosen on the basis of the similarity of sales volume in 1965 between these firms and the companies in the sample of government contractors. Generally, they were adjacent firms on the *Fortune* list of the five hundred largest industrial corporations in 1965. Each group reported an aggregate sales volume of $7.3 billion for the year. The general industry sample contained the following business firms: National Dairy Products Corp., Firestone Tire and Rubber Corp., General Foods, Aluminum Company of America, Colgate Palmolive Company, and Purex, Inc.

The two samples were compared, for the years 1962–1965, and

also for the earlier period 1952–1955, on the basis of standard financial ratios, traditional stockholder factors, and capital structure. A span of years was chosen in each case to reduce the effect of erratic movements in individual years.

The results of the analysis are contained in Table 2–3. It can be seen that government-oriented corporations tend to operate on much smaller profit margins than do typical industrial corporations—2.5 per cent versus 4.5 per cent during the years 1962–1965. As a result of the large amounts of government-supplied capital, which are not reflected on the books of these companies, the government contractors report a far higher ratio of capital turnover (that is, dollars of sales per dollar of net worth) during 1962–1965—almost seven times versus somewhat over two times.

TABLE 2–3 *Comparison of Government- and Commercially Oriented Corporations*

	Average of Sample of Government Contractors		Average of Sample of Commercial Firms	
	1962–1965	1952–1955	1962–1965	1952–1955
Financial Characteristics:				
Profit margin on sales	2.6%	3.0%	4.6%	4.5%
Capital turnover	6.8×	6.1×	2.3×	2.9×
Return on net worth	17.5%	18.6%	10.6%	13.0%
Investor Evaluation:				
Price/earnings multiple	10.9	7.3	20.6	10.7
Bond rating (Moody's)	Ba-Baa	Ba-Baa	A-Aa	A-Aa

SOURCES:*Moody's Industrial Manual,* 1952–1955 and 1962–1965; company annual reports, 1952–1955, 1962–1965.

The higher turnover rates for the government contractors more than offset their lower profit margins. Hence, their returns on net worth (net profits as a per cent of stockholders' investment) were considerably higher—17.5 per cent versus 10.5 per cent during 1962–1965.[39]

Moreover, the differences between the two samples widened over the past decade. As shown in the table, the sales margins of the government-oriented corporations were closer to the general industrial sample during the earlier period (1952–1955) than during the more recent years analyzed (1962–1965). The same trend is noticeable for the other financial measures, capital turnover and return on investment.

Despite the greater relative profitability, the evaluation by the stock market of the government-oriented corporations has been less favorable than of large business firms as a whole. This results, at least in part, from the inherent instability of the government market and the historical volatility of the fortunes of individual contractors. Reflecting these factors, earnings of defense companies tend to be more fully discounted, as shown by lower price/earnings multiples—eleven versus twenty-one for the period 1962–1965. (The results for 1952–1955 were not substantially different.)

Similar investor reluctance towards government-oriented corporations is evident in the bond market. Of the six firms which composed the general industry sample during the period 1962–1965, four were able to issue bonds with the relative high ratings of A or Aa (according to the standard Moody's bond rating); one chose not to issue bonds at all; and the last placed its bonds privately.

Out of the six companies in the government sample, only one issued bonds on the market and these had relatively low ratings of Ba and Baa. One of the firms placed its bonds privately, while the other four did not issue any at all. Again, the results for 1952–1955 were similar. These comparisons suggest that it is much easier for civilian-oriented firms to enter the bond market on favorable terms. It would be expected that this reflects the greater degree of risk which is imputed to bonds issued by government contractors.

An attempt to sum up the growing differences between government-oriented and commercially oriented corporations yields a paradox, but perhaps not an unexpected one. The close dependence of the government contractors on the volatile military customer results simultaneously in higher average profitability and

lower investor interest. The higher profitability arises mainly because of the free provision of working and fixed capital. The lower
stock and bond market evaluation comes about, in part at least,
because of the greater volatility of military requirements and,
hence, of the fortunes of individual contractors.

Another factor influencing investor attitudes may be the inability of these companies to operate successfully in commercial
markets because of their preoccupation with government requirements. Certainly other large government contractors—such as
General Electric, Radio Corporation of America, Honeywell, General Motors, Ford, and American Telephone and Telegraph—
which receive the bulk of their sales and income from consumer
and industrial markets encounter more favorable investor attitudes. With reference to Professor Galbraith's forecast of the
possible disappearance of that line between the mature corporation and the state, the market at least seems to distinguish increasingly clearly between government-oriented and commercially oriented corporations.

Some Policy Alternatives

Recent periods of defense cutbacks gave rise to demands for
utilizing the allegedly unique research and development and
systems management capabilities of military contractors in civilian public sector activities. Some precedents exist, but of a fairly
specialized nature. The design and production of space systems
for NASA are an outgrowth in part of military ICBM programs.
Likewise, the development of a supersonic transport aircraft
under the sponsorship of the Department of Transportation is an
extension of military aircraft developments. In both cases, the
companies involved in working on these civilian public systems
are long-term military contractors (North American Rockwell,
McDonnell Corporation, Boeing, General Electric, and others).
Indeed, the current concern over the need to respond to the
racial problems in the centers of the nation's major cities has
resulted in renewed pressures for putting to work the science

and intellect of our major high-technology corporations in the fields of education, training, mass urban transportation, urban redevelopment, and the reduction of poverty generally. Already, major aerospace companies have begun to penetrate emerging "systems" markets in the civilian public sector, such as oceanography, environmental pollution control, and the development of a commercial supersonic aircraft. Given another reduction in military spending in the near future, such action may also be an effective short-term means of preventing unemployment in defense areas. However, as a matter of long-term public policy, would it be wise for the nation to expand that branch of industry which increasingly develops the characteristics and mentality of a government arsenal? On the basis of the preceding examination of the government-industry relationship, it would appear at the least that important adverse side effects may arise and need to be dealt with.

Some of these side effects result from the adoption of well-established military contracting procedures by civilian agencies that are unaccustomed to buying complex systems. Also, their contracting personnel ("buyers") tend to obtain their training and initial experience with military procurement offices, which historically have represented the largest source of federal demand for purchasing personnel.

To a considerable degree, the major government contractors rarely risk large amounts of their own resources in new undertakings, but primarily respond to the initiatives of the governmental customer. This course of action may be a valid profit-maximizing solution for these companies, but it hardly promotes the risk-bearing and entrepreneurship which is characteristic of private enterprise. Should we encourage these companies to expand into civilian government markets in the same type of protected or insulated environment? Or should more emphasis be given to the possibilities of encouraging, or at least not discouraging, the eventual movement of personnel, facilities, funds, and other resources to those other industries which are more accustomed to operating in a commercial business rather than a government environment? Perhaps an added and unnoticed benefit of arms reduction would be the opportunity to reduce the "semi-nationalized" nature of this branch of the American economy.

Even in extended cold war periods, the "convergence" tendencies of government contractors may need to be held in check in order to maintain their present high rate of technological innovation which forms such a basic part of the nation's national security base. An important justification of the government-oriented (and, hence, publicly assisted) corporation is that it is in a position most readily to undertake scientific and technological innovation. Yet, innovation is likely to come forth only if there remains some risk of not innovating due to competitive pressures. Such pressures may come from existing government suppliers as well as from companies now oriented to commercial markets.

What reasonable steps can be taken to improve the situation? The following policy suggestions share one common characteristic: they are designed to reduce the close and continuing connection between the federal government and a relatively small group of industrial firms. By reducing both the governmental orientation of these companies and the government's reliance on them, the nation might be able simultaneously to achieve several important objectives—reducing the geographic concentration of federal contracts, increasing competition for government business, protecting the interests of the taxpayer, and reducing the arsenalization of an important branch of American industry. That is quite a tall order and the following points are not offered as a definitive solution, but as important initial steps in the right direction.

One way of reducing the financial dependence of defense companies on the government would be to make interest on working capital an allowable cost on military contracts. Interest on indebtedness is a standard cost of doing business and should be recognized as such. Unlike the period of rapid and uncertain expansion of defense work in the early 1940's, military contracts are now an established feature of American industry. The Treasury no longer needs to serve as banker.

A second way of strengthening the private entrepreneurial character of defense firms is to streamline and reduce the variety and scope of special provisions in procurement legislation and regulations. Let defense companies develop their own safety rules to discourage employees from skidding on factory floors. We seem at times to forget why in the first place we prefer to use private enterprise rather than government arsenals to develop and produce most of our weapon systems. It is not because private corporations are better than government agencies at following rules and regulations—at doing it by the numbers. It is precisely for the opposite reason. We hope that private enterprise is more creative, more imaginative, and more resourceful.

A third way of reducing the close, continuing relationship between the military establishment and its major suppliers is to broaden the competitive base. This could be accomplished by encouraging commercially oriented companies to consider military work as a possible source of diversification for them. The recommendations concerning interest on working capital and streamlining procurement procedures should help on that score. Also, defense companies could be encouraged to diversify into commercial markets. It may be natural for procurement officials to favor firms whose interests are not "diluted" by commercial work. However, the diversified company may also be the more efficient one in the long run. Certainly, the diversification of industry both into and out of the military market would reduce the present tendency for a relatively small number of companies to become primarily dependent on military business.

Another method of broadening the competitive base would be to emphasize production rather than research and development as the major point of competition. This could be done by doing more of the design work in federal laboratories and making the designs available to the various private companies who would bid on the production work. Substantial precedents exist for this approach. NASA did the primary development work on the

Saturn rocket booster, and subsequently they commissioned private industry to produce the boosters. Alternatively, the design and development work could be done in the private sector, with the companies competing for this kind of work not being permitted to bid on production contracts.

At present, much of the military subcontracts go to companies that are prime contractors on other systems. More attention in the award of subcontracts could be paid to small business and other industries not actively participating in the military market as primes. Some thought also could be given to reducing the competitive advantages that accrue to the dominant primes that hold on to government-owned plant and equipment for long periods of time. The free provision of these assets also explains their high profit rates. The simplest approach, of course, would be to curtail the practice of furnishing plant and equipment to long-term government contractors and, instead, to give them greater incentives to make their own capital investments.

Some Guidelines for the Future

The optimal in government-supplier relationship, therefore, may be substantially short of either arsenalization or the informal contact of a free market. The desired result may be enough stability to assure technical competence but enough uncertainty to prod some mutual participation in the innovation process.

Hence, it would appear that governmental procurement policies and practices need to be modified in order to halt the erosion of the basic entrepreneurial character of the firms that undertake large-scale developmental programs for government agencies. The plea for "disengagement" made by government contractors to the military establishment may need to be given greater weight, although the public interest would necessitate continuing protection and concern.

In any event, some second thoughts may need to be given before we as a nation agree to the almost uncritical demands for extending the use of these government-oriented corporations to other parts of the public sector. Rather, the current interest in utilizing American industry in dealing with the problems of urban areas may need to be tempered by the realization that simultaneous steps need to be taken to avoid the unintended but undesirable side effects which can result from close, continuing industry-government working relationships.

Certainly, the detailed day-to-day governmental surveillance of internal company operations which is so characteristic of the military weapon system market would appear to be a poor precedent to follow in establishing the relative roles of industry and government in such civil public sector areas as urban rehabilitation, environment pollution control, and training and education.

On the positive side, governmental procurement of goods and services from the private sector might well emphasize the end results desired by governmental decision-makers, rather than the detailed manner in which industry designs and manufactures the final product. In its essence, this is the difference between detailed design specifications prepared by the governmental buyer versus clear statements of performance desired by the government. The latter approach gives maximum opportunity for private initiative and inventiveness to come to bear on the problems of the public sector.

That, of course, is the basic and difficult task of using private enterprise in the performance of public functions without either converting the companies to unimaginative arsenalized operations or letting them obtain windfall profits because of the government's inability to drive hard and intelligent bargains.

The approach that is suggested here is neither so dramatic as a slashing attack on any military-industrial complex nor so simple as mere opposition to a war machine. Rather, these modest suggestions are both more constructive and somewhat more likely to be adopted. Although it will be difficult to obtain, that subtle balance between government and business interests which would strengthen simultaneously both the national defense and the private enterprise system needs to be sought.

NOTES

1. Don K. Price, *Government and Science* (New York: New York University Press, 1954), p. 92.
2. An earlier version of some of the following analysis is contained in Murray L. Weidenbaum, "Arms and the American Economy: A Domestic Convergence Hypothesis," *American Economic Review*, Vol. LVIII, No. 2 (May 1968).
3. Andrew Shonfield, *Modern Capitalism: The Changing Balance of Public and Private Power* (New York: Oxford University Press, 1965), pp. 341–346.
4. Walter Adams, "The Military-Industrial Complex and the New Industrial State," *American Economic Review*, LVIII, No. 2 (May 1968), 652–665.
5. John Kenneth Galbraith, *The New Industrial State* (Boston: Houghton Mifflin Company, 1967), p. 393.
6. *Ibid.*, pp. 392–394.
7. Murray L. Weidenbaum, "The Federal Government as a Buyer," *Journal of Purchasing*, I, No. 3 (November 1965), 14.
8. *Survey of Current Business*, July 1968, p. 37.
9. Some of the following analysis is drawn from Murray L. Weidenbaum, "Concentration and Competition in the Military Market," *Quarterly Review of Economics and Business*, Vol. VIII, No. 1 (Spring 1968).
10. Department of Defense, *100 Companies and Their Subsidiary Corporations Listed According to Net Value of Military Prime Contract Awards*, Fiscal Year 1967; National Aeronautics and Space Administration, *Annual Procurement Report*, Fiscal Year 1967.
11. U.S. Congress, House, Committee on Appropriations, *Hearings on Department of Defense Appropriations for 1963*, Part 4 (Washington, D.C.: U.S. Government Printing Office, 1962), p. 19.
12. William L. Baldwin, *The Structure of the Defense Market 1955–1964* (Durham: Duke University Press, 1967), p. 117.
13. Armed Services Procurement Act, 10, United States Code 2301–2314.
14. U.S. Congress, Senate, Select Committee on Small Business, *The Role of Small Business in Defense Missile Procurement—1958*, Hearings before a Subcommittee, April 29–May 1, 1958 (Wash-

ington, D.C.: U.S. Government Printing Office, 1958), p. 59.

15. Department of Defense, *Military Prime Contract Awards and Subcontract Payments and Commitments,* July 1965–June 1966, p. 36; National Aeronautics and Space Administration, *op. cit.,* p. 9.

16. U.S. Congress, Joint Economic Committee, *Economy in Government,* Part 1 (Washington, D.C.: U.S. Government Printing Office, 1967), p. 9.

17. Carl Kaysen and Donald F. Turner, *Antitrust Policy: An Economic and Legal Analysis* (Cambridge: Harvard University Press, 1959), p. 30.

18. Joe S. Bain, *Barriers to New Competition* (Cambridge: Harvard University Press, 1956), pp. 195–196.

19. U.S. Congress, Senate, *Economic Concentration,* Hearings before the Subcommittee on Antitrust and Monopoly of the Committee on the Judiciary, Part 1 (Washington, D.C.: U.S. Government Printing Office, 1964), p. 231.

20. Edward J. Morrison, "Defense Systems Management: The 375 Series," *California Management Review* (Summer 1967), p. 17.

21. George E. Pake, "Basic Research and the University's Future," *Washington University Magazine* (Fall 1967), p. 5.

22. National Science Foundation, *Basic Research, Applied Research, and Development in Industry, 1964* (Washington, D.C.: U.S. Government Printing Office, 1966), p. 73.

23. David E. Bell *et al., Report to the President on Government Contracting for Research and Development,* April 30, 1962.

24. Stanford Research Institute, *The Industry-Government Aerospace Relationship* (Menlo Park, Calif.: Stanford Research Institute, 1963), II, 119.

25. U.S. Congress, House, Committee on Appropriations, *Department of Defense Appropriations for 1968,* Part 4 (Washington, D.C.: U.S. Government Printing Office, 1967), p. 401.

26. Department of Defense, *Selected Economic Indicators,* February 1968.

27. Armed Services Procurement Regulation, Section E–503.

28. *Ibid.,* Section 15–205.17.

29. *Code of Federal Regulations,* 41, Chapter 18 (December 1967), Vol. XXXII, No. 223, Paragraph 18–1.112.

30. Cited in George Steiner and William G. Ryan, *Industrial Project Management* (New York: Macmillan Company, 1968), p. 79.

31. *Ibid.,* p. 80.

32. Armed Services Procurement Regulation, Sections 3–900, 1–800,

1–707, 7–203.8, 6–100, 3–800, 1–1700, 12–601, and 12–102.3.

33. Michael D. Reagan, *The Managed Economy* (New York: Oxford University Press, 1963), p. 193.
34. Armed Services Procurement Regulation, Section 7–600.
35. *Ibid.*, Section 3–902.1.
36. *Ibid.*, Sections 1–323, 1–327.1, 1–315, 15–205.31, and 15–205.33.
37. Department of Defense, *Defense Industry Bulletin* (November 1967), p. 22.
38. Steiner and Ryan, *op. cit.*, p. 145.
39. Additional comparisons were made between the sample of defense companies (which covers virtually the total universe of data) and large American industrial corporations generally (based on the *Fortune Directory* of the 500 largest U.S. industrial corporations). The results were similar to those reported here. For 1962–1965, the aggregate profit margin for the top 500 was 4.8 per cent, the capital turnover rate was 2.1, and the return on net worth was 10.0 per cent.

3

<hr>
<hr>

DIVERSIFICATION INTO
PUBLIC SECTOR MARKETS:
REDUCING COMPANY DEPENDENCE
ON THE MILITARY ESTABLISHMENT

The newest and perhaps the fastest growing aspect of contracting out the performance of government activities to the private sector involves the use of the major defense contractors, that is, the government-oriented corporations, in the programs of domestic welfare agencies. From the viewpoint of these companies, the civilian agencies provide potential market diversification. For the agencies, these high-technology private companies provide capabilities not present in the government's own work force. From the viewpoint of society, the results and implications are far more subtle and mixed; the growing involvement of industry in the government's business brings complication and concern as well as new resources.

Early Defense Industry Diversification Efforts

A brief historical analysis of the diversification efforts of the major defense contractors can provide considerable insight into their current interest in and potentials for serving civilian public sector programs.[1]

Post-World War II Burst of Enthusiasm

Ever since they attained the production peaks of World War II, the major military contractors have been concerned with the problem of diversifying into new markets and new types of production in order to maintain and expand the scale of their operations. The older and more established industries, such as automobile, rubber, and steel, which had originally converted from civilian markets, experienced little difficulty in returning to their traditional lines of business when the war was over. Backlogs of pent-up demands and accumulated wartime savings made this transition relatively easy.

In contrast, however, the specialized defense contractors—notably those in the aircraft industry—had typically grown during the wartime period from small job-shop operations to large industrial enterprises. The virtual or at least temporary disappearance of their basic market when the war ended brought fundamental problems of adjustment. The numerous efforts these companies made to expand into other businesses were characterized by diversity, enthusiasm, and confusion. One among numerous examples of the naïveté of some of these efforts was contained in the recommendation by a prestigious consulting firm to one large aircraft producer that it manufacture pesticides for farmers. The basic justification apparently was on theological grounds: "anything that stays the hand of pestilence is fundamentally sound."

Some of these efforts were frankly designed to take immediate advantage of a temporary demand for consumer items which had been missing from the economy during World War II. Other efforts were designed to utilize the substantial cash reserves accumulated during the war and to help tide the companies over during the reconversion period. Some of the defense companies began producing buses, trolley coaches, marine engines, aluminum canoes, and sport boats, which required their skills in fabricating light metal products. Some of the related products were a bit far afield from their customary areas, including bottle labelers, coin changing machines, dry cleaning apparatus, artificial hands, and midget racing cars. Among the most imaginative efforts was the production of coffins, both stainless steel and aluminum.

Several defense firms became subcontractors for established companies in commercial markets. In that role, they built heater cases, parts for musical instruments, automobile components, plumbing, cabinets for radios, and water tanks for railway cars. One company bought into a consumer finance agency in order to prepare for the postwar boom in private aircraft that never materialized.

In general, the income from these new ventures was disappointing. They did not generate a significant fraction of the sales attained during World War II; the profits were often negative. This was illustrated by the experience of the major aircraft companies during the initial postwar adjustment period, 1946–1948, when sales declined to a tenth of their former peak and losses totaled over $50 million.

Most of the diversification activities by the major, specialized defense contractors which were begun at the end of World War II were abandoned as unsuccessful or marginal or sold to firms traditionally oriented to industrial or consumer markets. The expansion of the military budget brought on by the Korean War soon turned the primary attention of these firms back to the military market. When faced with the alternative, few aircraft companies preferred to manufacture powered wheelbarrows or buses rather than bomber or fighter airplanes.

Post-Korean Industrial Diversification

The end of the Korean War, of course, sparked another round of interest in commercial diversification on the part of defense contractors. These efforts attempted to take account of some of the worst mistakes of the past, bypassing particularly the consumer markets which had proven to be so alien to the high-technology defense-oriented firms.

The largest diversification efforts were represented by the closest adaptations of military work—aircraft for the airline and executive markets. The other diversification projects also typically were limited to industrial markets. These included industrial electronics, small gas turbine engines, nuclear reactors, wall panels for commercial buildings, and heavy-duty land vehicles. Despite the variety of these latter efforts, the nongovernment sales of the major aircraft companies during the middle 1950's were almost entirely transport aircraft delivered to the commercial airlines.[2] Most of these industrial diversification efforts outside of aerospace fields have since been abandoned. The surviving diversification programs continue generally at marginal levels—either actually losing money, barely breaking even, or at best showing profit results below typical military business returns.

Reorientation in Defense Industry Diversification

During the late 1950's and early 1960's, the interest and attention of the high-technology companies that primarily serve the military market were focused predominantly on the expanding military and closely related space budgets. The cutbacks in 1963–1964 in military procurement programs, particularly for large missile systems, produced a reorientation of defense industry thinking on diversification, a shift with particular significance for the civilian parts of the public sector.

Several reexaminations of the previous diversification efforts of defense contractors, as well as new evaluations of their peculiar strengths and weaknesses, led to the awakening of their interest in doing work for government agencies other than the military establishment.[3] The success of the leading defense firms in gaining the major NASA contracts was an important indication of their ability to use their engineering and scientific skills in other government markets. That significant and successful diversification within the government market also showed that it was not the ability of defense producers to fabricate light metals (shades of aluminum and stainless steel coffins) which was their primary competitive characteristic. Rather, it was their scientific and systems management capability which enabled them to develop and penetrate new markets. In their search for additional civil public sector business, the new market often had to be established and developed before it could be penetrated. That is, the potential contractors for civilian public sector systems not only had to convince the government customer that they had the ability to perform as promised, but that the very undertaking itself was something that the government, rather than private enterprise, should sponsor and fund.

Evaluating the Obstacles to Diversification

In evaluating the diversification efforts of the major defense contractors, it is helpful to consider these undertakings from a broader view than merely entrance into commercial markets.

In terms of diversification within military and related high-technology government markets, these firms have been eminently successful. The shift from aircraft to missiles and space systems ranks as a noteworthy accomplishment in the development and sale of new products (See Table 3–1). Moreover, this latter type of diversification also met such basic and important business standards as high return on investment, increase in the growth rate of the enterprise, and effective utilization of surplus resources and capabilities. This is a striking contrast with their commercial experience.

A variety of explanations is given by students of the defense industry for the inability of the large specialized government contractors to use their capabilities successfully in commercial endeavors. The principal reasons for past failures fall into two major categories: lack of management motivation and lack of required capabilities.[4]

TABLE 3–1 *Market Diversification of Aerospace Companies*

Customer	Per Cent of Sales								
	1960	1961	1962	1963	1964	1965	1966	1967	1968
Department of Defense	76	77	75	71	64	55	54	58	55
National Aeronautics and Space Administration and other government	2	4	7	13	18	22	20	15	14
Commercial aerospace	13	10	9	7	10	14	15	17	22
Nonaerospace	9	9	9	9	8	9	11	10	9
TOTAL	100	100	100	100	100	100	100	100	100

SOURCE: Aerospace Industries Association.

The lack of management motivation, it appears, is due to such basic factors as their belief that strong incentives to change are absent. This is bolstered by their feeling that commercial opportunities are inadequate. Thus, defense company personnel who are concerned with reorienting their operations to more traditional lines of industry obtain limited interest or support from management. These factors are cumulative and interacting.

The absence of incentive results in good measure from the belief of the top managements that there are adequate sales opportunities in government work and that the profit rates are, if anything, higher than on risky commercial ventures (some evidence to bear this out was presented earlier). Interviews with chief executives of the defense industry repeatedly brought out their firm belief in the long-term nature and rising trend of the military market. Also, their many prior unsuccessful diversification attempts have engendered a strong conviction that inadequate commercial opportunities exist for companies which have become oriented primarily to government work. The following quotations from interviews with defense industry chief executives are typical:

There is nothing to convert to; it is all a matter of marketing, timing and being able to commercially exploit the technology and you can't legislate it . . . you can't make them buy it.

There are darn few applications requiring high level technology. It is easier to escalate technology than to depress it.[5]

The defense industry failures at commercial diversification would fill a large chamber of horrors.[6] One company acquired a plastics research firm and subsequently closed down the operation. Another large defense contractor began producing metal-curtain wall panels, lost money, and discontinued the venture. A third defense company acquired firms manufacturing mobile homes, reported operating losses, and subsequently sold the entire line of business. One of the companies also began and subsequently abandoned an effort to penetrate the industrial computer business. The unsuccessful commercial diversification efforts literally ranged from canoes to computers to coffins. As a result, there has been in most cases very limited management support for or interest in diversification. This is evidenced by the few investments made in comparison with more traditional military or airline projects. Another indication is the reluctance to commit full-time senior management or top technical personnel to these diversification ventures. Again, the statements of defense industry executives are revealing:

Diversification would dilute management's effort on the basic product line.

Management believes that it should devote its energy and money to what we are doing and what we know how to do.

The second set of reasons for unsuccessful commercial diversification relates to the specialized capabilities of these government contractors. These firms—compared with commercially oriented companies—have relatively low capitalization, little if any commercial marketing capabilities, and limited experience in producing at high volume and low unit cost. Moreover, their entire administrative structure is geared to the sometimes unique reporting and control requirements of the governmental customer.

The low capitalization of the large defense corporations—the relatively small amount of stockholders' investment in relation to sales volume—was shown earlier. A related problem is that the traditionally low price-earnings ratio of the stock of these companies limits their ability to diversify through merger; because their stock is so often selling at a discount compared to commercially oriented companies, a merger would dilute the equity of existing shareholders.

The lack of commercial marketing experience is a familiar refrain in defense industry circles. One company president has stated that "it's not a merchandising industry." A typical comment of another chief executive evoked the same theme: "Lack of knowing the market prevents us from coming up with a salable product, even though we could compete with the established companies on a technical basis."

Because of the more specialized nature of military equipment, there is less emphasis on volume production at low unit costs. Rather, these firms are used to producing at close tolerances and high quality, under great pressure from the governmental customer to develop even more advanced equipment. Meeting that last 1 per cent of military specifications may be very expensive, but essential. In contrast, in commercial work the company usually starts off with broader specifications and then trades off continually between improving the product and lowering the cost. Thus, firms used to the environment of weapon system design and development may not have developed the cost orientation needed to perform and compete successfully in commercial markets. As one defense industry executive put it, "Our company doesn't know how to cut corners well enough."

A new model of refrigerator at half the price of current types may have a large market even if it suffers from significant reductions in quality. The second best missile, in contrast, may hardly be a bargain. The comparison of course is oversimplified. Nevertheless, it illustrates the different nature of product innovation characteristic of commercial competition as compared to technological competition in the military field.

It is thus not hard to understand why defense company managements are so reluctant to move from fields they have mastered into lines of business quite alien to them. Their lack of knowledge of nondefense industries is pervasive. It includes ignorance of products, production methods, advertising and distribution, financial arrangements, funding of research and development, contracting forms, and the very nature of the private customer's demands.

Clearly, the type of company that can successfully design and build a new multibillion dollar ICBM network or space exploration system has a capability differing from that of the soap, steel, toy, or other typical cost-conscious but low-technology company operating in the commercial economy.

Even if we examine companies that have both weapon system and commercial product divisions, we find little transference of either personnel or product ideas from government to commercial work within the same firm. A company's commercial departments may be hiring engineers, while simultaneously a military department may be laying off experienced technical personnel.

Available surveys show that large proportions of the engineers and scientists who leave a company doing military work go to other firms similarly engaged in government contracts. There has been considerable movement of professional and technical personnel from universities and nondefense industries to government work, but relatively little movement in the opposite direction. Differences in pay scales and degree of challenges in the work are often cited as barriers to movement from government to commercial work.

Hence, the key resources of the government-oriented corporations—their management and their scientific personnel—become locked-in and further dependent on the governmental customers. Every failure at commercial diversification and equally every successful governmentally contracted undertaking serves to accentuate the locked-in nature.

A More Positive Approach

Despite the negative findings of the previous section, a positive approach to utilizing the capabilities of defense contractors in other areas may still be possible. A balanced appraisal of a company's or industry's true assets and liabilities should be made in relation to the tasks to be undertaken. The seller's lack of a vast distribution network is of little concern to the military customer which maintains a substantial system of supply depots of its own. The lack of mass production experience is of limited interest to a civilian space agency responsible for the design and development of relatively few numbers of new, scientifically advanced systems. Rather, the absence of these unneeded commercial-type capabilities may tend to keep overhead down and to orient the company to uniquely meeting the needs of its traditional government customers.

What then are the positive resources of the large, specialized defense contractors? Clearly, their engineering design and development capability is especially strong. The work forces of these companies often approach being primarily large aggregations of scientists, engineers, and supporting technicians. Compared with the most technically oriented industry serving commercial markets, such as drugs or chemicals, the typical defense company may have four or five times the number of scientists and engineers to support a given volume of end-item sales.[7] The top managements of many of the leading aerospace companies, for example, are dominated by engineers—McDonnell-Douglas, Boeing, Lockheed Aircraft Corporation, and so forth. Clearly, the specialized defense contractors possess strong capability to perform research extending the state-of-the-art, as well as preparing complex engineering designs. Related to that attribute is a management that is capable, some say uniquely capable, of managing the development, production, and integration of large and complex systems; this ability is often termed "systems management."

Similarly, these companies possess positive but specialized production capabilities. They are experienced at producing high-value items incorporating advanced engineering and scientific design. A related manufacturing asset is the ability to work with exotic materials and to close tolerances.

Despite the numerous lamentations concerning their lack of marketing ability, these firms have been most successful in penetrating one large and rapidly growing market area—government business. In fact, they have experienced unparalleled success in selling complex systems involving advanced technology to a select governmental clientele. Their knowledge of defense and space markets, customer requirements, and public contracting procedures is detailed and often authoritative.

Hence, a balanced appraisal does yield some positive strengths on the part of the government-oriented corporations—their striking engineering and scientific talent for developing new products and services, their systems management capability, and their knowledge of how to serve government agencies. It is not surprising thus that the most recent diversification efforts of these government-oriented companies have been into newly emerging, high-technology markets within the public sector itself. Here there is little fear of competition from firms entrenched in the market, nor is there need for the elaborate merchandising and distributing required for many commercial markets. Rather, here is where the government-oriented corporation may find itself at a strong advantage. Nevertheless, the development of new markets, as we shall see, is full of pitfalls as well as potentials.

Defense Companies and Public Sector Markets

From a national viewpoint, the utilization of defense-space capabilities in other parts of the public sector possesses considerable attraction. It would represent a useful civilian return on this primarily security-related investment and also would help to meet other national objectives. From the viewpoint of the individual company, such public sector diversification would reduce its dependence on two fairly closely related government markets—defense and space. Finally, by using the by-products of the basic defense-space product lines, the nation as well as the companies would be getting an added return on an investment which already has been made and has been written off.

The California Experiment

One of the most ambitious efforts to utilize defense contractors and defense technology, certainly the most widely publicized program, consisted of four exploratory contracts awarded by the state of California in late 1964 and early 1965. The impetus for these contracts came from the 1963–1964 reductions of military orders for large missile and related aerospace weapon systems, the mainstay of the state's large defense industry. The plans were ambitious, particularly in view of the relatively small size of each contract—$100,000. The Lockheed Aircraft Corporation was chosen to design a statewide information handling system and to develop a plan for its implementation. North American Aviation was charged with developing a work program indicating the content and specifications for a systems approach to solving basic transportation problems. Aerojet-General Corporation received two of the contracts. One was to explore the feasibility of applying systems engineering and operations analysis techniques to social problems and to recommend a program for prevention and control of crime and delinquency. The other was to assess the suitability of the systems approach and related analytical tools for solving California's waste management problems.

Each of the companies spent more than $100,000 on the assigned study, thus investing some of their own funds into the effort. Thus, they also postponed to a later date the possibility of breaking even in this new area of business, much less earning a profit. Inevitably, a flow of reports resulted from the four contracts. How successful were they? The evaluations that have been made yielded mixed results.

There were several frequently voiced criticisms of the four studies. Some contended that they were weak in their knowledge of the subject matter, as evidenced by incomplete or incorrect data, as well as inadequate knowledge of the pertinent literature or the state-of-the-art. Others maintained that the recommendations were politically naïve and impractical to implement. Another complaint concerned the overemphasis on engineering and insufficient attention to social, political, and administrative aspects.[8]

The most basic criticisms related to the naïveté of defense industry personnel, which led them to think that they could blithely apply the so-called systems approach as readily to social, political, and economic questions as they had to military problems. The president of one aerospace company was quoted as saying, "Creating a system to warn a field army the enemy has launched an attack of germ warfare is basically no different from creating a system to control juvenile delinquency."[9] Or, to parody Gertrude Stein, a system is a system is a system. There also comes to mind that probably mythical manual that listed three types of security: internal security, port security, and social security!

Apparently the four systems' studies attempted to accomplish too much in too little time. Each of them thus wound up in recommending that the state subsequently undertake follow-on programs, costing at least $1 million a year. To date, none of these follow-on programs have been implemented. This may be explained in part by the fact that, although the four contracts were paid for by the state of California, the program was financed to a substantial degree by funds that were federal in origin.

Perhaps the most negative evaluation of these efforts was made by Professor Bruce Smith of Columbia University, who has studied in some detail the attempts of the federal government to contract out programs involving advanced technology. Professor Smith concluded that the California experiment "was misconceived from the start." He maintains that the policy questions were posed in a biased way to begin with. "The State said, in effect, that certain technological resourses (i.e., and aerospace industry) were in danger of being underemployed, and therefore how could these resources be used in solving state problems?" The emphasis, he maintains, should be reversed: to start with the problems to be solved and then to see what use could be made of the technology.[10]

On the positive side, most of the publicity was favorable, if not uncritical. In his analysis of this particular aspect of the contracts, John Gilmore concludes that "the studies were successful."[11] Harold Walt, who at the time was a senior California state official dealing with the four exploratory contracts, reported as noteworthy that the state attracted the attention of industry to its problems and that industry thus also made the state aware of its capabilities.[12] It may be indicative of this new government-industry relationship that two of the companies that received contracts established offices in the state capital, which they did not have previously.

As a result of the $440,000 expenditure by the state for the four initial studies and related consulting work, California has received about $1 million in federal funds to support five additional systems studies. These cover a criminal justice information system, planning information for waste disposal, land use planning data, and an examination of public assistance systems. Some of these research funds were utilized by state agencies; the great bulk was contracted out to defense companies.

In a more general way, all of the original contractors, as well as other defense firms, have expanded their civil sector systems activity since the completion of the initial California effort. Most are performing work for a variety of state, local, and federal government agencies. Aerojet-General Corporation received two additional contracts from the state of California, but neither was a direct follow-on to its earlier work.[13]

The Demonstration Effect

The at least temporary cutbacks in military procurement in 1963–1964, and the demonstration effect of the California experiment encouraged many other defense contractors to seek business in the parts of the public sector they had previously ignored. Although the dollar volumes of these undertakings are still small judged by the scale of military and space programs, they do involve government agencies now doing business with high-technology private enterprises that were originally attracted to government work by the military establishment. Some nondefense firms have also begun to seek contracts in these newly emerging public sector markets.

The present appears to be a period of substantial exploration on the part of both government agencies and business enterprises in assessing the kinds of relationships through which they can successfully do business with each other. Table 3–2 indicates some of the variety of recent contracts awarded by civilian government agencies to the government-oriented corporations. In most cases, these business-government relationships did not exist as recently as five years ago. It is, hence, too early to judge the successes or failures, or even to judge with great confidence the long-term trends that may be developing. However, on the basis of experience to date, four areas stand out as civilian public sector activities where the type of systems analysis and advanced technology possessed by the leading military-space contractors can usefully be involved: transportation, water systems, communications systems, and regional development.[14]

Transportation

Innovations in the area of transportation which have been suggested as potential endeavors for defense contractors include mass urban transportation networks, integration of existing surface systems, highway safety and traffic control, modernizing the merchant marine, and developing an alternative to the passenger automobile for personal transportation. In some of these cases, the most difficult barriers may not be technological at all, but rather political, social, and institutional.

A current example of innovative transportation work by a government-oriented corporation is the development by Lockheed Aircraft Corporation of a transportation plan for the Sudan. This work is being undertaken through contracts with the Agency for International Development and the Sudan's Ministry of Finance

TABLE 3–2 *Typical Civilian Public Sector Contracts*
Awarded in Recent Years

Subject	Governmental Customer	Corporate Contractor
Auto safety	New York State	Fairchild-Hiller
Campus design	St. Louis junior colleges	McDonnell-Douglas
Classroom scheduling	St. Louis junior colleges	McDonnell-Douglas
Desalinization plant design	U.S. Department of Interior	Lockheed
Education information system	city of Philadelphia	Philco-Ford
Education information system	state of California	Aerojet-General
Educational reference center	U.S. Office of Education	North American Rockwell
Educational technology	U.S. Department of Education	Lockheed
High speed ground transportation	U.S. Department of Transportation	Hughes Aircraft
High speed ground transportation	U.S. Department of Transportation	TRW, Inc.
Information system	state of Alaska	Lockheed
Information system	state of California	Lockheed
Information system	state of Massachusetts	Lockheed
Instrumentation research	U.S. Department of Transportation	Melpar
International development	Agency for International Development	Lockheed
Medical information system	state of Vermont	TRW, Inc.
Parcel sorter	U.S. Post Office	Aerojet-General
Power management system	U.S. Department of Interior	North American Rockwell
Regional development	Department of Commerce	Litton
Satellite communications	Comsat Corporation	Northrop
Supersonic transport aircraft	U.S. Department of Transportation	Boeing
Supersonic transport engines	U.S. Department of Transportation	General Electric
Systems analysis of poverty	state of Colorado	Philco-Ford
Traffic control system	New York City	Sperry-Rand
Transportation system design	state of California	North American Rockwell
Turbines for ground transportation	U.S. Department of Transportation	United Aircraft
Waste management	state of California	Aerojet-General
Waste management	U.S. Public Health Service	Aerojet-General
Zip code reader	U.S. Post Office	Philco-Ford

SOURCES: Denver Research Institute and Washington University NASA Economic Research Program.

and Economics. In its systems analysis of Sudan transportation, Lockheed is charged with developing a broad plan for development of all forms of transportation, indicating specific projects and establishing priorities among them.

Within the United States, TRW, Inc., is conducting detailed engineering studies of transportation requirements for the country's Northeast Corridor. The company is evaluating, for the Department of Transportation, alternative modes and travel concepts which can be used in a safe and convenient high-speed ground-transportation network.

At the more specific product level, United Aircraft has built an experimental "Turbo Train" under sponsorship of the Department of Transportation, for the Penn-Central Railroad. Made mostly of aluminum and other light-weight materials, and powered by aircraft-type gas turbine engines, the Turbo Train is designed to provide high-speed comfortable surface transportation to help alleviate the airport and highway congestion problems of the Northeast Corridor.[15] Similarly, the Bell Aerospace subsidiary of Textron, with the assistance of funds from the Department of Housing and Urban Development, has developed an "air cushion" vehicle, the *Jet-Skimmer*. It is being used to take passengers from the Oakland and San Francisco airports to downtown San Francisco and across the Bay via a quick water route—in contrast to a lengthy drive on the California freeways.[16]

Clearly, the systems type of public transportation market in the United States is in an early developmental state. The governmental funding generally is in terms of hundreds of thousands of dollars, characteristic of exploratory study phases, rather than the contracts in units of tens of millions which are associated with actual production of operational systems.

Water Systems

The suggestions that have been made for the application of defense industry science and technology to public sector activities in the water area vary from mining of the ocean floor, and sea farming, to salt and brackish water conversion on a commercial scale and effective water pollution control systems for entire watershed areas. In many instances there are important questions of benefit-cost analysis to be answered, particularly regarding the allocation of the benefits and costs to specific groups and industries. Substantial obstacles to government action may be present, for example, in those cases where the cost of pollution controls is expected to be borne entirely by localities upstream on a river, but where the benefits entirely accrue to residents in downstream localities. These are not simple questions, nor are the solutions readily available. They may require public policy decisions of a very subtle nature before markets for industry develop to a significant degree.

At a less ambitious level, several government-oriented corporations (Aerojet-General Corporation, General Dynamics Corporation, McDonnell-Douglas, and United Aircraft) have been testing to determine whether waste water can be reclaimed through "reverse osmosis" (filtering out impurities with thin membranes). The General Dynamics Corporation has been working with sanitation authorities in Los Angeles County and the city of San Diego. Westinghouse Electric Corporation is under contract with the state of Pennsylvania to determine whether techniques used for desalting water can be employed to purify acid mine drainage, a major source of stream pollution.

As in the case of innovation in transportation, the use of government-oriented corporations to develop new water systems has been quite limited. To date, there is little indication of effective demand on the part of government agencies both willing and able to award large-scale contracts. Rather, the efforts thus far mainly indicate some of the future potentials for government agencies drawing upon the technological resources of the private sector.

Communications

Numerous specialized communications applications come to mind as possible public sector diversification on the part of companies now primarily working on defense contracts. Custom-designed communications could enable the individual schools in a given district to utilize a single set of specialty teachers. Such networks also could link the outlying field offices and divisions of a large government agency or department. A worldwide satellite relay system is another possibility and would be an outgrowth of the existing communications satellite (Comsat) spin-off from government space programs. Still another possibility is the establishment of a truly effective communications system for a single large institution, such as a hospital or a prison—cases where improved information may lead directly to improved decision-making capability. A variety of potential public customers is apparent here, including state, local, and federal as well as foreign governments.

Many defense-space contractors have obtained civilian government contracts in which modern computer technology is drawn upon to improve communication systems, notably in the areas of education, health, and justice. For example, Aerojet-General Corporation has been working with the California Department of Education on a computer system for evaluating teacher credentials. This should reduce the time required to review all teacher applications. General Precision Systems, Inc., is developing closed circuit, on-site telecasts for schools via a mobile video control room. The mobile facilities can shoot and process the film, and broadcast the results to remote monitors. The McDonnell-Douglas Corporation has used its Automation Center to do the physical planning for the St. Louis junior college district. By achieving more efficient space utilization patterns, the computer analysis yielded a 100,000 square feet reduction in the proposed building plan and a cost saving of over 20 per cent out of a $13.5 million construction budget. The McDonnell Automation Center has done work for a variety of other public and private clients, including county, state, and federal agencies, hospitals, religious institutions, and companies in numerous manufacturing and service industries.

At a more ambitious level, several major defense contractors have set up new units to penetrate the public education field through teaching machines and related software. LTV, Inc., has acquired three business colleges to form a division of its new subsidiary LTV Education Systems, Inc., and to provide a proving ground for its computer-assisted instruction, automated teaching aids, and other new educational technology.[17]

Several defense contractors are actively attempting to develop improved communication systems for hospitals. TRW, Inc., did the systems analysis for a $100 million medical complex in Alberta, Canada, including designing and developing fully integrated communications, logistics, and information handling systems. The Mayo Clinic of Rochester, Minnesota, has retained the Lockheed Aircraft Corporation to study the speed of flow of medical information, seeking to free doctors from time-consuming routine. That company is also providing a computerized disaster casualty management system for the Texas Hospital Association. The University of California at Los Angeles has been using in its medical research a computer program originally created by North American Rockwell for use in solving a variety of rocket engine vibration and combustion problems. In the area of crime control, Northrop is under contract with the state of Pennsylvania to develop a criminal justice information system; it began with a study of the requirements for a description of a recommended information system and will go on to develop a plan for implementation.[18]

On a broader scale, defense contractors are designing statewide communications systems intended to streamline the flow of information and reduce the continuous demand for personnel. Such systems are being developed for such state governments as Alaska, California, and West Virginia. It appears that the public sector activities involving computer technology and information-handling systems are currently the most promising technical areas for involving the government-oriented corporation. In many of the cases, the work contracted goes beyond preliminary exploration and frequently proceeds to the point of actually installing operational systems and equipment.

Regional Development

The possibilities for applying defense industry technology and systems concepts to area or regional development are numerous and far-reaching. They range from technical assistance to developing nations overseas and urban renewal and redevelopment in our major metropolitan areas to conceptually as well as geographically new housing and community development projects ("New Towns" or "Satellite Cities"). Related alternatives include industry-operated educational and training centers.

The most far-reaching attempt thus far to apply systems analysis to the economic development of a region is the contract with the government of Greece under which Litton Industries has committed itself not only to analyze and plan the growth of agriculture, industry, and commerce in an underdeveloped area (Crete and Western Peloponnesus), but actually to attract new investment to it. This project indicates the potentially wide-ranging role of systems contractors doing government work.

In part because of the adverse international image that the current Greek regime projects in some quarters, the investment goals ($60 million of outside investment in two years) were not realized. Only $27 million of firm commitments were reported during the first 23 months and few of these projects have yet been launched. On reflection, the attraction of long-term capital would be expected to be a relatively slow, drawn-out affair.[19]

Litton Industries' undertaking in Greece is one of the few diversification projects for which some profit data are available. The company receives costs plus an 11 per cent profit on its economic studies and 1.9–2.25 per cent of the equity capital or long-term foreign loans that it attracts to Crete or the Peloponnesus. However, numerous misgivings over the project have been expressed from a broader viewpoint of public policy: How desirable is it for a large American corporation to be under contract with a foreign military dictatorship with the objective of strengthening the economic base of such a regime? This is clearly a question with important political ramifications which are difficult for an individual profit-seeking business enterprise to take account of in any meaningful way. The Litton Industries experience also indicates the wide-ranging potential role of systems contractors in doing government business. Litton Industries itself has entered into somewhat similar arrangements with Portugal and Turkey. Northrop has contracted with Iran to revamp irrigation and transportation systems.

Within the United States, several defense firms have begun to do work in the urban field, an area of growing public concern. On a much less ambitious level, General Electric's center for advanced studies, TEMPO, is working with the city of Detroit to introduce budgeting techniques learned through its cost-effectiveness work on projects for the Department of Defense. That company is also involved with the University of Minnesota on an experimental city to be built near Minneapolis.

Ten major government contractors (Aerojet-General Corporation, Control Data Corporation, Emerson Electric Company, Litton Industries, Ralph M. Parsons, American Cement Company, Northrop, TRW, Inc., Raytheon, and Lockheed Aircraft Corporation) formed a consortium early in 1968 to apply aerospace technology to urban problems. The organization, Urban Systems Associates, Inc., was headed up by two retired Air Force generals and was launched with considerable fanfare. Not too surprisingly, it got off to a slow and shaky start. By the end of the first year, four of the companies had dropped out. Aerojet-General Corporation, Litton Industries, and TRW, Inc., all decided to go it alone. Raytheon determined that it was not yet ready for the urban market. No specific undertakings by the consortium have yet been announced.[20]

In a more specific but no less ambitious way, the OEO has awarded Westinghouse Electric Corporation a special contract to develop a comprehensive program to attack all the problems of a designated slum area in Baltimore.[21]

Several large companies have been operating Job Corps camps

for the federal government's anti-poverty program. The General Learning Corporation, a joint venture of General Electric and Time, Incorporated, is operating a Job Corps center in Clinton, Iowa. International Telephone and Telegraph is operating the center in Camp Kilmer, New Jersey, and Thiokol Chemical Corporation the one in Clearfield, Utah. Philco-Ford is cooperating with the University of Oregon to manage the Job Corps installation in Astoria, Oregon. In a somewhat related effort, General Dynamics Corporation, Litton Industries, and Westinghouse Electric Corporation are running Peace Corps training stations in the United States. For example, General Dynamics Corporation leased a Girl Scout camp near San Diego to use as a center where Peace Corps trainees are learning Hindi and farming techniques before going to rural villages in India to help increase agricultural yields.[22]

In view of rising national concern with the complex of racial and poverty problems that are centered in the major urban areas, it is likely that the relatively small undertakings just described will, in coming years, grow into large-scale government utilization of private industry. Already, many public and private figures have urged the formation of new types of government industry partnerships in order to rebuild in a fundamental way major portions of the central cities of our largest metropolitan areas.

A Preliminary Evaluation

It is not hard, thus, to work up considerable enthusiasm for the nation's obtaining some civilian return on its massive investment in military and space programs through the type of undertakings in transportation, communication, hydrology, or urban systems described above. Nevertheless, upon some reflection, a number of significant caveats come to mind.

From the viewpoint of the individual companies, are these types of projects likely to lead to profitable lines of business in the long run? So far, it does not appear that they have. If substantial profitability is not achieved in the years ahead, is there likely to be a day of reckoning resulting in a complete industrial disenchantment with or revulsion from the government as a customer? From the vantage point of the government agency, does the continued and increasing contracting out of government programs tend to reduce the effectiveness of public control over the use of public funds and the conduct of government programs? From the point of view of the average individual, will government become even more remote with the interposition of a private contractor between the government itself and the ultimate beneficiary? Visions of people caught between two large bureaucracies —one public and one private—with almost infinite buck-passing capabilities conjure up demands for new types of ombudsmen that could create a novel growth labor market.

Finally, for society as a whole, would the close working relationships between the ostensibly private companies and government agencies result in accelerating the trend towards arsenalization of industry which already seems visible in the defense area? Given the anticipated rapid growth in civilian public expenditures in coming decades, would at least some of the locus of entrepreneurship, initiative, and risk-bearing shift from the private to the public sector of the American economy?

Certainly, these serious but unintended impacts of government-industry relationships need to be taken account of in a major way prior to any wholesale utilization of the government-oriented corporations for designing, developing, and producing new and large-scale systems for the civilian public sector.

Perhaps, technology will produce its own limits. For example, some of the enthusiasts in the defense industry for the application of the systems concept seem to have gone so far as to almost invite an inevitable reaction. Perhaps the ultimate in their naïveté is a formal technical paper presented by an engineer from a large aerospace company in which he contended that the defense industry systems concept could usefully be applied to football.[23]

NOTES

1. This section draws upon material in "Aircraft Makers Diversifying," *Business Week*, September 28, 1946; Murray L. Weidenbaum, "Product Diversification in Aircraft Manufacturing Industry," *Analysis Journal* (May 1959); and Murray L. Weidenbaum, "Problems of Adjustment for Defense Industries," in Emile Benoit and Kenneth Boulding, eds., *Disarmament and the Economy* (New York: Harper & Row Publishers, 1963).

2. U.S. Congress, House, Committee on Armed Services, *Aircraft Production Costs and Profits* (Washington, D.C.: U.S. Government Printing Office, 1956), p. 2725.

3. See *Changing Times in the Defense Industry* (Washington, D.C.: Electronics Industries Association, 1964).

4. Murray L. Weidenbaum and A. B. Rozet, *Potential Industrial Adjustments to Shifts in Defense Spending* (Menlo Park, Calif.: Stanford Research Institute, 1963).

5. The quotations in this section are taken from *ibid.*

6. *Ibid.*, p. 31.

7. U.S. National Science Foundation, *Research and Development in Industry, 1966* (Washington, D.C.: U.S. Government Printing Office, 1968), p. 73.

8. John S. Gilmore *et al.*, *Defense Systems Resources in the Civil Sector* (Washington, D.C.: U.S. Government Printing Office, 1967), p. 43; Elliot F. Beideman, "State Sponsorship of the Application of Aerospace Industry Systems Analyses for the Solution of Major Problems of California" (Ph.D. diss., University of Southern California, 1966).

9. *Wall Street Journal*, June 9, 1965, p. 1.

10. Bruce L. R. Smith, "The Future of the Not-for-Profit Corporations," *Public Interest* (Summer 1967), p. 137.

11. Gilmore, *op. cit.*, p. 40.

12. Harold Walt, "The Four Aerospace Contracts: A Review of the California Experience," in *Applying Technology to Unmet Needs*, Appendix, Vol. V: *Report of the National Commission on Technology, Automation, and Economic Progress* (Washington, D.C.: U.S. Government Printing Office, 1966), p. 51.

13. Gilmore, *op. cit.*, p. 46.

14. Murray L. Weidenbaum, "Strategies for Diversification of Defense-Space Companies," in American Marketing Association,

1967 June Conference Proceedings (Chicago: American Marketing Association, 1968); and Aerospace Industries Association, *Aerospace Technology: Creating Social Progress* (Washington, D.C., 1968).

15. Paul W. Burton, "Testing the Turbo Train," *United Aircraft Bee-Hive* (Spring 1968), pp. 10–15.
16. *Vertical World* (August 1966), p. 5.
17. *Saturday Review*, July 23, 1966, p. 34; McDonnell Automation Center, *Automation: A Catalyst for Growth* (St. Louis, undated); Eli Goldston, "New Prospects for American Business," *Daedalus* (Winter 1969), p. 100; *Business Week*, February 1, 1969, p. 68.
18. *Diversification News*, August 29, 1966, p. 1; *Business Week*, October 29, 1966, p. 110; *Boston Globe*, November 27, 1966.
19. *Wall Street Journal*, February 20, 1968, p. 32, and September 10, 1968; George P. Baker, *New Markets for Business in the Public Sector* (Cambridge: Harvard University, undated) p. 9; *Industrial Research* (November 1968), pp. 27–28.
20. William H. Gregory, "Several Firms Planning Urban Programs, but Sales Prospects Are Vague," *Aviation Week*, July 1, 1968, p. 38 *et seq.*
21. Monroe W. Karmin, "Great Society, Inc., U.S. Seeks to Expand the Role of Industry in Tackling Urban Ills," *Wall Street Journal*, December 15, 1967, p. 1.
22. "Business Teaches the Peace Corps," *Business Week*, October 22, 1966, pp. 133–138; *St. Louis Post-Dispatch*, October 20, 1966; John McHale, "Big Business Enlists for the War on Poverty," *Trans-Action* (May-June 1966), pp. 3–9.
23. Roy B. Carpenter, Jr., *Football—A Systems Challenge* (American Institute of Aeronautics and Aeronautics Paper No. 66–896, December 1966).

4

ATTEMPTS TO USE NEW MECHANISMS

Along with its reliance on the government-oriented corporation, the federal government has been experimenting with several newer mechanisms whereby programs of national concern can be conducted essentially outside of the federal establishment itself. These organizational innovations—many of which reflect more the pressing needs of the moment than any carefully planned and structured organizational approach—include the direct establishment of new intergovernmental agencies, the encouragement of quasi-private organizations, and the reliance on existing private institutions as "fiscal intermediaries."'

Intergovernmental Organizations

Regional arrangements are beginning to take on greater importance in the federal system. These innovations range from such relatively long-term institutions as the Appalachian Regional Commission, set up by special act of Congress, to special purpose conferences established for various more limited, short-term pursuits. This "new regionalism," as it has been called, is thus far resulting in only the mildest shift in the locus of power and concern to subnational levels.[1] However a noticeable increase is occurring in the involvement of both the federal government

93

and the states in the planning of new programs as well as in their execution.

The most ambitious regional effort to date results from the attempts to deal with the multi-state problem of lagging or "distressed" areas of the nation, where Congress has established several regional economic development commissions. These commissions represent an attempt to develop new machinery whereby the federal government and the states can deal cooperatively with problems of mutual concern. Although the successes of the substantive programs have been limited to date, the mechanisms themselves—neither wholly federal nor wholly local—seem to be quite promising.

Each of the six regional commissions established to date is a hybrid organization consisting of the governors of the states involved plus a federally appointed commissioner. The result is that the commissions are neither purely federal nor state instruments.[2]

In an attempt to protect the national interest, the federal representative's vote is required, along with a majority of the governors, for any action by these commissions. Similarly, each governor on a commission has a veto power over what will be done in his state; only he can bring proposals before the commission for implementation in his state. This "liberum veto" apparently has not resulted in paralyzing the organizations as supposedly was the effect on the old Polish Parliament, when each member could veto legislation.

In establishing the commission for the Appalachian region, Congress gave it the comprehensive responsibility for devising a strategy for developing Appalachia, as well as substantial powers over federal funds appropriated to put its plans into effect. The Appalachian Regional Commission has allocated the funds to the states, not on the traditional basis of population or area alone, but also on their evaluation of need. Hence, Kentucky and West Virginia, with the most underdeveloped transportation facilities, have received the bulk of the highway construction money. Similarly, Pennsylvania has received the lion's share of mining area reclamation funds, because it contains the most serious problems in that category.

Ralph Widner, the Executive Director of the Appalachian Regional Commission, states that there have been no attempts at the commission's meetings to impose a federal point of view or for states to form a bloc. Rather, he contends, the commission has developed stands on many issues which are neither a state nor federal position, but one which has been developed jointly by the two, and which becomes binding on both.[3]

Similar commissions, although with substantially less funding, have been established for New England, the Ozarks, the Upper Great Lakes, the Coastal Plains, and the Four Corners area of the Southwest. The operations of these regional commissions, which merit further study as they develop, represent an important innovation in the American federal system. They represent a significant effort to bring together the states and the federal government in joint efforts which use the superior financial resources of the United States Treasury but depend on the organizational and administrative capabilities of the states.

In some respects the regional commissions other than the Appalachian agency are subject to federal budgetary and administrative control. The Secretary of Commerce must approve their administrative budgets. The federal government also provides administrative and support services to all of the commissions on a centralized basis. These services include procurement, mail and messenger, transportation, library, graphics, printing and reproduction, accounting and auditing payroll, budgeting and financial reporting, recruiting, personnel record keeping, legal and public information, and office space. One observer describes the commissions as "but a facade of intergovernmental cooperation."[4] Nevertheless, the Appalachian agency and its sister commissions represent an innovation in our federal system which already has attracted substantial interest as a prototype for future governmental action in dealing with domestic problems of wide scope.

A major shortcoming is the narrow scope in which these regions are defined. In focusing on the problems of lagging economies, most of these regions have been drawn to exclude the large metropolitan areas which, at least economically, are a vital part of the area. For example, the Ozark Commission excludes St. Louis. In the future, should the regions served by the economic development commissions be broadened to include the adjacent metropolitan areas, then they may well serve as the framework for a fundamental revision in the federal system: an intermediate layer of governmental authority between the federal government and the fifty states.

Quasi-Private Organizations

As was noted earlier, the national security agencies have depended heavily on contracts with business corporations for the design, development, and production of most of the weapon systems and other equipment that they require for carrying out their missions. Perhaps a more striking development has been the extent to which the federal government has fostered the creation of nonprofit organizations, nominally in the private sector of the economy, which receive the bulk of their funds from the federal government.

In general, when we think about private, voluntary nonprofit organizations in our society, we are prone to conjure up thoughts of the Red Cross, the Elks or the Knights of Columbus, or the endowed private museum or college—all examples which are clearly neither governmental in their concern nor businesslike in their operation. The so-called nonprofits that we are concerned with here are legally of the same nature as the benevolent societies, but they are more in the nature of hybrids; their operation more closely approximates a blend of the government agency and the private business concern.

The military establishment has used private nonprofit organizations (Rand Corporation, the Institute for Defense Analyses, and the Research Analysis Corporation, among others) to provide an independent systems analysis capability. Such nonprofit institutions (Aerospace Corporation and Mitre Corporation) also have been utilized for the more delicate task of monitoring and guiding the work of industrial contractors.

An early civilian-oriented example, and a precedent for the largest one in the fields of education and poverty reduction, was the demonstration programs started in 1961 in sixteen cities by the President's Committee on Juvenile Delinquency and Youth Crime. Federal grants were made to either local government agencies or private nonprofit groups. Most of the demonstration projects were run by newly created, private, nonprofit, nongovernmental agencies.[5]

More recent examples are the twenty regional educational laboratories which were set up soon after the Elementary and Secondary Education Act of 1965 provided for federal funding of such private ventures. A letter from former President Lyndon B. Johnson to then Secretary of Health, Education, and Welfare, John W. Gardner, clearly indicated the federal role:

> I look to these laboratories . . . to build links with other Federal programs. . . . Thus the laboratories should be related to the supplementary centers provided for in the Elementary and Secondary Act of 1965, to the teacher training programs of the Office of Education and the National Science Foundation, to appropriate activities of the Office of Economic Opportunity and the National Institutes of Health.
>
> I congratulate you and those who helped you to develop the concept of these laboratories and request that you give continuing attention to their effective development.[6]

Typical of the twenty regional laboratories is the Central Midwestern Regional Educational Laboratory, incorporated as a private not-for-profit organization in November 1965. It is governed by a board of directors made up of fifty educational, civic, labor, and business leaders of a four-state region surrounding St. Louis. Using mainly federal funds, the laboratory attempts to improve the effectiveness of local public and private schools by developing and encouraging the application of new educational methods and concepts.

The extent to which it acts as an agent of the federal government can be seen in the following excerpt from the laboratory's bylaws:

> The purposes of the organization are . . . to implement all aspects of Public Law 89–10, Title IV, and such other titles, as are appropriate for the planning and operation of an educational laboratory operating as part of the National Program of Educational Laboratories authorized by Public Law 89–10, Title IV. . . . To implement any and all appropriate aspects of any subsequent legislation related to, complementing, extending, or in any way modifying the National Program of Educational Laboratories authorized by Public Law 89–10, Title IV.[7]

The Board of the Central Midwestern Regional Educational Laboratory adopted a policy statement that, where feasible, the organization should seek funds from outside of the federal government. Along these lines, the Danforth Foundation provided an initial planning grant, and affiliated educational institutions (local school systems and colleges) have made modest contributions. However, the permanent board of directors was not selected until after the United States Office of Education had approved a substantial grant establishing the regional laboratory as part of its national program.[8]

Similarly, the OEO has drawn upon or encouraged the creation of a variety of local agencies in order to administer at grass roots levels the funds appropriated to help eliminate poverty in the major urban and rural areas of low income and high unemployment. Geographically, these are much smaller areas than those dealt with by the regional economic development commissions. Because of the greater amount of resources available to it, the anti-poverty program has resulted in a variety of political and institutional conflicts over the locus of control over funds, personnel, and program. The major focus of the war on poverty—

the Community Action Program—is basically a direct federal-local program, largely bypassing the states but also, with its stress on involvement of private groups, de-emphasizing the role of local government.

This bypassing is sometimes deliberate, in order to circumvent state and local government establishments that are not sympathetic to, or at least do not wish to take responsibility for, the changes that these federal programs attempt to bring about (for example, school integration and open housing). Over three-quarters of the more than 1,100 community action agencies, which receive most of their support from the OEO, have been established as private nonprofit organizations.

According to OEO regulations, the local community action organization "must be broadly representative of the interests of the community." Frequently this requires going beyond the elected governmental officials to obtain the participation of the key minority groups who are the major intended beneficiaries of the program. In many cases, especially in the South, local officials have not wanted the primary responsibility for such a program aimed at upsetting the status quo. However, in many cases they are willing to cooperate with and even serve on a new, nonprofit private organization encompassing various community groups, including labor, business, and welfare institutions.

The structure of and control over the community action agencies have been evolving. The original legislation gave governors an absolute veto on community action programs, as well as several other OEO activities, notably Job Corps centers and neighborhood Youth Corps projects, within their state boundaries. Amendments adopted in 1965 modified this power and permitted the director of OEO to bypass the gubernatorial veto "for good and sufficient reasons."[9]

In the original legislation, the role of local government units was also played down. By March 1966, however, OEO moved to recognize the role of local government by instructing its regional offices that elected city or county officials could veto all or any part of the proposals of a community action agency within their jurisdiction. In late 1967, Congress gave local governments the responsibility for establishing or designating these agencies for participating in the anti-poverty program. OEO must also approve the designation. If state or local governments fail to create or designate a "satisfactory" agency, the OEO may select a private nonprofit organization for this role. In practice, the amendment has brought little change in local control of community action programs. As of the fall of 1968, only twenty-two out of eight hundred agencies surveyed by OEO had been taken over by local governments. Four others had switched to private administration.

Congress also specified the standards for the composition of the governing boards of the community action agencies. At least one-third must be representatives of the poor, "selected by democratic procedures." Up to one-third must be public officials, if they are willing to serve, and the remainder must be selected representatives of various interest groups—business, labor, religious, minority, welfare, education, and others.[10]

OEO also has established the controls over the personnel practices of these agencies. For example, it must approve any starting salary over $5,000 or promotion which involves a salary increase of over 20 per cent or $2,500. Also, no employee may engage in "partisan political activity."[11] While the federal government is authorized to assume the full cost of certain community action programs, the basic ratio of federal assistance to matching local contributions is set at 80–20 per cent (beginning July 1, 1967). The original legislation provided for a 90–10 per cent federal-local matching formula. However, the local contribution need not be, and typically is not, in the form of cash. They can be made "in kind"—work space, heat, power, or volunteer services.[12]

Since the beginning of the program, there have been noticeable cutbacks in the amounts of local initiative permitted. In late 1965, for example, OEO ordered its regional directors and the managers of local community action programs to weed out "low priority" and "low quality" projects. OEO itself specified six areas which the local agencies were to consider as low priority:

educational counseling and guidance, remedial education, all "in-school" education, recreation and camping, cultural enrichment, and social science counseling. In addition, OEO specified that manpower development projects and multi-purpose neighborhood centers should be given high priority by the ostensibly private local community action agencies.[13] Although the priorities determined by OEO might have made good sense, the limited amount of local and private initiative was indicated quite clearly.

If there is much question as to the extent to which the community action organizations are veritable agents of the federal government, that probably can be resolved by examining OEO's specifications for such organizations which may receive OEO recognition and funds. The specifications cover such items as particular functions to be performed (which range from family planning to voter education to consumer assistance), detailed methods of operation, personnel practices, salary systems, and methods of contracting for goods and services.[14]

Another OEO program, Project Upward Bound, presented during its development phase an even more vivid, although smaller, example of the close government-institute relationship. Project Upward Bound was essentially an attempt to create a "head start" program for teenagers, that is, to assist potential high school dropouts to complete their secondary education and go on to college.

In view of the great internal administrative difficulties that OEO experienced in setting up Head Start, it was decided to rely primarily on outside help in the newer Upward Bound project. In the words of the first director of Upward Bound, the policy was "to maintain a very small Upward Bound staff in OEO and delegate out to the Institute for Services to Education (ISE) in Pittsburgh most of the administration of the program."[15]

ISE is a nonprofit institution headed by a distinguished board of college presidents, deans, department chairmen, and other educators at Yale, Berkeley, Carnegie Tech, MIT, and other well-known universities.

The contract between OEO and ISE shows quite clearly the

extent to which the nominal private organization was to administer government functions and the government agency was to control the internal operations of the private organization.[16]

Under the contract, ISE was delegated the authority to prepare the guidelines and standards, as well as to design and distribute the forms and announcements, for Project Upward Bound. All of this was subject, of course, to OEO approval.

In addition, ISE was charged with evaluating the proposals that the agency would receive from the outside educational groups that would actually do the training. That this evaluation was more than nominal may be inferred from the provision of the contract requiring ISE to prepare the documents necessary for processing OEO grants. The personal contact that a college would have with Washington on its potential role in Upward Bound was an academic professional working for ISE. OEO, on the other hand, retained full control over the hiring and retention of all ISE's professional personnel working on Upward Bound. This gave it greater control over the personnel than if the program were operated "in house" with Civil Service personnel.

In part, as a result of strong attacks on the Upward Bound contract with ISE (covering such questions as lack of competition in the award of the contract and improper use of private personnel in performing government functions), Congress voted to transfer the project to the Office of Education beginning July 1, 1969.[17]

An interesting partial case of the close alliance between a private nonprofit institution and the public sector is the federal research and development centers generally operated by a university under a long-term, continuing relationship. Clarence Danhof has concluded that these centers represent the use of the contract mechanism to establish and operate facilities which, before World War II, would have been intramural organizations, if it had been possible for the federal agencies to establish them at all.[18]

The National Science Foundation straightforwardly reports

that these centers, "in most instances were established to meet a particular R&D need of a federal agency. . . . The supporting federal agency determines the objectives of these organizations. . . ."[19]

Examples of these federal contract research centers include the Applied Physics Laboratory at Johns Hopkins University, the Lincoln Laboratory at MIT, and the Lawrence Radiation Laboratory at the University of California, Berkeley.[20]

Danhof has identified some special characteristics which distinguish these centers from other types of research institutions:

1. All are managed by private institutions under contracts which have a marked continuity. Since 1946, some changes in contractors have occurred, but only a very few research centers have been disbanded.

2. The centers are closely identified with a single government agency. The bulk of the work of each center is done for one agency, which is its official sponsor.

3. The centers have contractual responsibilities for furthering the interests of the sponsoring agency in broad mission or program terms. All projects are assigned through administrative procedures rather than through competition with proposals submitted by possible alternative research and development groups.

4. Some restraints on personnel policies exist. The most common and important are provisions for reviewing the general salary structure, particularly salaries above a certain level—frequently $25,000 a year. Typically where the federal research and development centers are affiliated with a university, special employees, rather than regular faculty members, constitute the bulk of the employees.[21]

A more extreme case of the ostensibly private research and development facility which is closely allied to the federal government is the "sponsored, nonprofit organization," which the General Accounting Office has defined as "one for which a Government agency has assumed responsibility for providing sufficient work and revenues to ensure retention of acquired capabilities to meet Government needs."[22] In common parlance, these organizations, mainly used by the military establishment, have become known as "captives" of the federal agency which sponsors them.

In the years following World War II, the Department of Defense brought into being a number of such quasi-private, non-private, nonprofit companies to augment the in-house capabilities of the military services. According to the Air Force, it had not had sufficient time to build competence within its own organization, and Civil Service regulations made it difficult to quickly recruit staffs possessing the required capabilities.[23]

The first of these nonprofit corporations, managed by a group of private citizens constituting a board of trustees, was the Rand Corporation. A group originally was established at the Douglas Aircraft Company in 1946 to provide systems analysis through a Project Rand contract with the Army Air Corps. Despite the autonomy that the Douglas top management gave the Rand group, there appeared to be at least an incipient conflict of interest when one defense contractor, although at arm's length, provided special advice to the military customer on the selection of weapon systems, and then competed against other firms for the resultant contracts. From this group there evolved shortly thereafter the Rand Corporation which performed the mission with considerable skill. The technical success of this pioneering effort led to the creation of several other nonprofit corporations by defense agencies in the late 1950's and early 1960's.

The increased need for strategic analysis led to the formation in 1956 of the Institute for Defense Analyses, used by the Joint Chiefs of Staff and the Director of Defense Research and Engineering. In 1958, Analytic Services, Inc., was established to provide the Air Force a capability in analyzing the immediate problems which were not in the province of Rand. In 1961, the Army fostered the establishment of the Research Analysis Corporation to take over work formerly done for it by an adjunct of Johns Hopkins University. In the same year, the Logistics

Management Institute was established to do long-range studies of military procurement for the Assistant Secretary of Defense for Installations and Logistics.

During this period, the Air Force's need for systems engineering and technical management brought into existence another group of nonprofits. The Mitre Corporation was formed in 1958 to assist in developing electronic command and control systems. The Aerospace Corporation was set up in 1960 to take over from a subsidiary of TRW, Inc., a task which was becoming increasingly controversial for a profit-making firm to handle—providing technical direction over the private companies who were serving as Air Force contractors for the ballistic missile programs. In 1956, a large operating division of Rand was spun off as the System Development Corporation which specializes in computer information programming and processing.

In recent years several congressional investigations of these captive, military, nonprofit organizations appear to have resulted in a halt in both their number and their individual growth.

Several other federal agencies that require large amounts of research and development also utilize the "sponsored" nonprofit mechanism. The most recent innovation is the Urban Institute which, it is contemplated, will have a relationship with the Department of Housing and Urban Development for long range studies similar to that of the Rand Corporation with the Air Force.

The private-versus-public nature of these organizations is a matter of considerable controversy. The Air Force, for example, contends that because of their close and continuing relationship to it, the business aspects of these nonprofits must be open to Air Force scrutiny, "much as an actual Air Force operation."[24] The General Accounting Office reported to Congress that many nonprofits engaged primarily in government work operate "for all practical purposes as extensions or adjuncts of the Government" and recommended that they be considered as "quasi-public" and subjected to more government constraints than a profit-making organization.[25]

The nonprofits themselves in turn claim that they require substantial autonomy of operations in order to perform more effectively their function of providing independent, objective advice and information to the sponsoring government agencies. The Air Force contends that the financial accountability that it desires is not inconsistent with the freedom of thought and independence on technical matters that is expected of them. The delicate nature of this balance was described by the Comptroller General in reporting to Congress on his survey of the captive nonprofits (however, the ultimately public orientation came through clearly): "We believe that there must be a reasonable balance between control in the Government's interest and flexibility of operations in order for the organization to capably serve to the ultimate benefit of the Government.[26]

Alan Pifer, the president of the Carnegie Corporation, has called attention to the expanding role in American society of the various types of private nonprofit agencies, all of which he embraces in the category of "quasi nongovernmental organization."[27] Classified in the private sector of the economy, this relatively new entity has in many respects the appearance of the private, nonprofit enterprise and even some of the characteristics of the true voluntary association. Typically, it has a private board of trustees or directors that is supposed to govern it, and that, at least in theory, is ultimately responsible for its affairs. The members of its staff are private employees and not civil servants. It is not housed in a government building or located on federal property.

Yet, as we have seen in the case of the education, poverty, and defense programs, this type of organization serves important public purposes as an instrument of "government by contract." Perhaps most important, it was created as the result of federal legislative or administrative action in Washington, rather than on the initiative of private citizens. It is dependent financially for its very existence on Congress and on the particular federal agency to which it is related or by which it is sponsored. Its most active channel of authority, therefore, tends to run between its paid staff and a federal organization in Washington, and its program is likely to be heavily influenced by federal needs and regulations. Pifer concludes that "at bottom, its freedom of action, compared with that of a truly private organization is considerably restricted because the necessity for public accountability is built into its very nature." It is interesting to note Pifer's parenthetical lament, "If only the government learned how to *buy* services the way a private corporation does and not run the provider of the service."[28]

Fiscal Intermediaries

The Medicare program of the federal government, in addition to its substantive effects on the quantity and quality of health care made available to older persons, is also resulting in the use of a relatively new organizational arrangement—the utilization of private institutions as fiscal intermediaries between the federal government and the ultimate beneficiaries. Blue Cross and Blue Shield groups, which have become widespread private nonprofit but quasi-public institutions, serve as the principal financial "middle man" between the patients and the federal government. In other cases, private insurance companies exercise this role. As Herman and Anne Somers conclude in their detailed analysis of the workings of Medicare: ". . . The bulk of day-to-day operations work is performed mainly by private organizations. These administrative intermediaries have responsibility for receiving and reviewing bills from doctors, hospitals, and other providers of care, and making payments."[29]

For the fiscal year 1967, 57 per cent of the administrative funds for Medicare were disbursed to the fiscal intermediaries and cooperating state agencies, and only 43 per cent of the money was spent by HEW, the federal agency responsible for the program. It has been maintained that HEW does not itself do the work of the fiscal intermediaries because the complexity, variety, and high sensitivity of the health field make this politically impractical. In a sense, the political heat as well as the program responsibility must be spread. The direct involvement of both the states and the private sector seems to be necessary in order to obtain sufficient public understanding and support of the program.

As in the case of utilizing the government-oriented corporations, here, too, unintended side effects may present important problems in the future, if not in the present. As the federal government continues to engage in what Carl Stover has called "the delegation of public authority to private agencies,"[30] administrative authority becomes separated from ultimate responsibility in a similar way to the divorce of ownership from management in the typical large corporation. The rumbles of discontent in some of the Job Corps camps, both those run by industry as well as those by academia, underscore the problems arising where the citizen is "administered" by organizations remote from either the relatively personal control of the political process or the more impersonal but effective control of the marketplace.

The addition of a private bureaucracy in dealing with the individual citizen on specific public programs is a situation which does not arise in the national defense area, but is likely to be common in other public sector activities, particularly those dealing with social welfare, where private organizations are utilized as middlemen. An ombudsman may become particularly necessary to protect the individual citizen from arbitrary treatment by two sets of bureaucracies with built-in buck-passing capabilities.

Another side effect of the fiscal intermediary mechanism is similar to that resulting from defense contracts—the lack of an open market to determine prices through the interpersonal operation of the forces of supply and demand. Medicare, too, depends on administrative determination of the prices to be charged to the government. This shortcoming is compounded by the absence of the profit motive on the part of the typical nonprofit hospital, which gives it little incentive to respond to pressures to reduce costs and increase efficiency.

In few areas of economic activity (other than the high-technology government programs analyzed earlier) are payments virtually guaranteed for costs that are neither controlled by competition nor regulated by public authority and in which little incentive for economy can be discerned. Increasing attention is being given to prior budget review as a cost discipline in this area. Some claim that this method already has been discredited by overrigid application by some local government bodies. Another alternative being considered is the "target rate" concept, similar to incentive price contracting in military procurement. Under this concept a target cost is set based on the hospital's recent experience. If its cost turns out to be less than the target, the institution gets to keep a share of the underrun as an incentive bonus. If its actual expense is greater than the target, it will be reimbursed only up to a previously specified maximum.[31]

The trend for federal agencies to closely supervise and increasingly control the operations of its contractors, so apparent in the highly developed case of military contracting, is thus also noticeable in the much newer Medicare program. In analyzing the subject of dealing with the rising hospital costs, Robert Sigmund, the Executive Director of the Hospital Planning Association of Allegheny County, has made this significant observation: "If SSA [the Social Security Administration] must pay on the basis of individual hospital cost, then it must get involved in managerial review and assistance. The budget is the key starting point."[32]

It is tempting to draw parallels, perhaps closer than is warranted thus far, but not totally unwarranted, between the development of the government-oriented corporation in national security programs and the potential changes in the medical and nursing personnel and organizations pending services through the Medicare program.

It does seem clear, however, that the states are only one among an array of alternative mechanisms available to the federal government in carrying out national purposes. From the viewpoint of federal agencies, dealing with these private or quasi-private organizations which lack sovereignty may be an easier way to proceed ("easier" in a bureaucratic sense as more amenable to control).

From the larger viewpoint of society as a whole, there may be considerable merit in softening the tendency for the federal government to be such a dominating force. Bolstering the roles of the states and the cities may be a major alternative. As we will see in the next chapter, to some extent the state governments and federal agencies have become more closely interdependent, but not to the extent that has occurred in such more striking cases as the military and the government-oriented corporations.

A conceptually simpler but perhaps operationally more difficult alternative would be greater reliance on the private sector to meet the needs of society. Without returning to a laissez-faire condition, this approach would require greater reliance on indirect government incentives and inducements: tax reductions when necessary to pump enough purchasing power into the economy to maintain full employment; more liberal tax write-offs to encourage private training of unemployed and unskilled people; and reduced operation of some of the regulatory agencies to promote greater competition among business firms. However, it is easy to forget the abuses and shortcomings that led to the establishment and expansion of federal government activities since the advent of the New Deal.

Perhaps the best that can be anticipated is not the wholesale abandonment of federal government expenditure programs but their rechanneling and redesign to avoid the adverse side effects that are becoming more noticeable. The states and their subdivisions provide an attractive area for such analysis, which is covered in the next chapter.

A More Radical Alternative

An extreme variation of federal programs which would bypass government-oriented corporations, regional commissions, and quasi-private organizations, as well as most of the bureaucracies of federal or state and local governments, would be the various forms of "guaranteed annual income." These plans have been suggested in various fashions. Essentially, guaranteed annual income plans provide for the federal Treasury to pay directly to each eligible family an amount designed to ensure that they have sufficient money to maintain a designated minimum adequate living standard. The size of the payment and the incentive to earn income vary substantially among the different plans. The use of the money would depend entirely on the discretion of the individual recipients. No governmental (or quasi-governmental) organization would direct, influence, monitor, or audit the expenditures made by the individuals or families receiving the federal funds.

Some guaranteed annual income schemes would provide each family, regardless of its income, with a standard payment ("family allowance") from the Treasury—let us assume $3,000 a year, for example, as an illustrative standard. A more common form proposes that the federal government pay each family the difference between their actual earnings and a predetermined floor, say $3,000 a year, when their own earnings fall below the "floor" or "guarantee." The federal government would be filling whatever income gap each family incurs.

Another form is the "negative income tax." Under this approach, the federal government would pay families earning less than, say, $3,000 a year, a fraction of the difference but would not fill the entire gap. Hence, an incentive would remain to increase earned income because, unlike the $3,000 annual guarantee, families earning less than $3,000 a year would always be better off if they increase their own earnings.

Table 4–1 compares the workings of the major alternative forms of the guaranteed annual income. It is assumed, for simplicity, that the negative income-tax rate is 50 per cent for incomes below $3,000. That is, a family with no income would receive 50 per cent of the difference between zero and $3,000, or $1,500. Although in concept the negative income tax differs substantially from a standard income guarantee, in practice the difference depends on the rate. That is, a 50 per cent negative income-tax rate is halfway between a full income guarantee and doing nothing; a 75 per cent rate is three-quarters of the way to a full guarantee; a 90 per cent rate closely approximates a complete guarantee.

TABLE 4-1 *Alternative Forms of Income Guarantees*

Annual Family Earned Income	Government Payment			Total Income		
	Family Allowance	Guaranteed Annual Income	Negative Income Tax	Family Allowance	Guaranteed Annual Income	Negative Income Tax
$5,000	$3,000	$ 0	$ 0	$8,000	$5,000	$5,000
3,000	3,000	0	0	6,000	3,000	3,000
2,000	3,000	1,000	500	5,000	3,000	2,500
0	3,000	3,000	1,500	3,000	3,000	1,500

Some forms of the negative income taxes and other income guarantees would be additive. That is, the benefits paid would be in addition to existing welfare programs, although they would help to relieve pressures for more generous welfare activities. Some advocates of these plans, notably Professor Milton Friedman of the University of Chicago, would go further.

They view the new payment plans as substitutes for the large welfare bureaucracies which have grown up at all levels of government, and they consider programs such as the negative income tax as a means for reducing governmental "interference" in private decision-making.[33] Under Friedman's approach, the negative income tax would provide purchasing power to private individuals who, in turn, could purchase education, health, and other goods and services from the commercial economy. There is no guarantee, of course, that the individual recipients would spend the money for these purposes, and not on entertainment, recreation, liquor, and similar "noninvestment" activities.

The basic approach of relying more heavily on private enterprise and individual choice is extremely attractive to many observers. The gnawing question remains to some—would the federal money be wasted (in any objective sense) and thus the underlying problems of illiteracy, joblessness, despair, and the recurring cycle of poverty remain?

At this time, it seems quite clear that the federal government is exploring a variety of mechanisms, some quite innovative and others milder adaptations of historic means, in an effort to carry out more effectively the growing array of responsibilities being thrust upon or assumed by it. Certainly, no individual mechanism emerges as the single, all-purpose means of conducting the government's business. Perhaps, an organizational pluralism is to be expected in our federal system. Some observers of this trend have voiced concern over the possible dangers to the federal system of government. The combination of federal and private power, it is contended, further reduces the role of state and local systems in the American form of government.[34] Certainly, the government-oriented corporations, intergovernmental organizations, and quasi-private institutions are all alternatives to the two more traditional methods available to the federal government in carrying on its functions: direct operations on the part of federal civil servants and cooperative ventures via grants-in-aid to state governments and their subsidiaries.

With this thought, it is appropriate to turn to still another aspect of the involvement of the federal government with the rest of the economy in carrying on its mission. The state and local governments represent major potential along these lines, potential which has already been tapped to some important extent.

NOTES

1. Daniel J. Elazar, "Continuity and Change in American Federalism," *Proceedings of the Sixtieth Annual Conference on Taxation* (Pittsburgh: National Tax Association, 1967), p. 20.

2. This section draws upon a seminal paper by Ralph Widmer, "The Future of Federalism" (A paper presented before the 25th Anniversary Conference, Union for Democratic Action Educational Fund, Inc., Arlie House, Warrenton, Virginia, October 8, 1966).

3. *Ibid.*, pp. 12–13.

4. Randy Hamilton, "The Regional Commissions: A Restrained View," *Public Administration Review*, XXVIII, No. 1 (January, February 1968), 21.

5. Advisory Commission on Intergovernmental Relations, *Intergovernmental Relations in the Poverty Program* (Washington, D.C.: U.S. Government Printing Office, 1967), p. 28.

6. Cited in Central Midwestern Regional Educational Laboratory, *Central Midwestern Regional Educational Laboratory, Inc. for Educational . . . Research, Innovation, Diffusion, Implementation* (St. Ann, Missouri, n.d.), p. 4.

7. Central Midwestern Regional Educational Laboratory, Inc., *Progress Report to U.S. Commissioner of Education on Contract O.E.C.–6–000535–0535* (St. Louis, Mo., April 1, 1966).

8. *Ibid.*, p. 3.

9. Robert W. Schleck, *Antipoverty Programs Under the Economic Opportunity Act* (New York: Tax Foundation, Inc., 1968), p. 17.

10. Office of Economic Opportunity, *Organizing Communities for Action* (Washington, D.C.: U.S. Government Printing Office, February 1968), pp. 7–8.

11. Office of Economic Opportunity, *Personnel Policies and Procedures*, Community Action Program Memorandum No. 23–A (August 26, 1966), Parts B and C.

12. Schleck, *op. cit.*, p. 18.

13. *Ibid.*, p. 27.

14. Office of Economic Opportunity, *Designation and Recognition of Community Action Agencies Under the 1967 Amendments to the Economic Opportunity Act*, Community Action Program Memorandum No. 8 (February 15, 1968), Part B.

15. Richard T. Frost, "Project Upward Bound" (unpublished paper, Washington, D.C., December 1968).

16. Office of Economic Opportunity, *Contract No. OEO–658* (October 1965).

17. *Congressional Record* (July 24, 1968), pp. H7412–H7416.

18. Clarence H. Danhof, *Government Contracting and Technological Change* (Washington, D.C.: Brookings Institution, 1968), p. 375.

19. U.S. National Science Foundation, *Scientific Activities at Uni-*

versities and Colleges, 1964 (Washington, D.C.: U.S. Government Printing Office, 1968), p. 32.

20. *Ibid.*, Appendix B.
21. Danhof, *op. cit.*, pp. 314–315, 375–376.
22. Comptroller General of the United States, *Need for Improved Guidelines in Contracting for Research with Government-Sponsored Nonprofit Contractors*, Report to the Congress B–146810 (February 10, 1969), p. 3.
23. *Ibid.*, p. 13.
24. *Ibid.*, p. 16.
25. *Ibid.*, pp. 45, 48.
26. *Ibid.*, p. 62.
27. Alan Pifer, "The Quasi-Nongovernmental Organization," *Annual Report, 1967* (New York: Carnegie Corporation, 1967).
28. *Ibid.*, p. 6.
29. Herman M. Somers and Anne R. Somers, *Medicare and the Hospitals: Issues and Prospects* (Washington, D.C.: Brookings Institution, 1967), p. 32.
30. Carl F. Stover, "The Government Contract System as a Problem in Public Policy," *George Washington Law Review*, XXXII (1964), 707.
31. Somers and Somers, *op. cit.*, p. 193.
32. Cited in *ibid.*, p. 250.
33. Milton Friedman, *Capitalism and Freedom* (Chicago: University of Chicago Press, 1962), Chapter XII.
34. Elazar, *op. cit.*, p. 21.

5

STATE PERFORMANCE AND
FEDERAL FINANCING

For the growing variety of low-technology domestic welfare programs that it authorizes and finances, the federal government has come to rely increasingly on states and their subdivisions for the actual conduct of the activities. The most striking examples are the federal budget categories for education, commerce, and transportation, where substantially more than half of the funds are disbursed in the form of grants-in-aid to state and local governments. Federal payments to local school districts account for the bulk of the national government's education outlays (61 per cent in the fiscal year 1967). Similarly, federal-aid highway and airport systems receive the largest shares of expenditures for commerce and transportation (57 per cent in fiscal 1967).

The largest concentration of federal grants to the states and localities is found in the health-labor-welfare category, where they reached $7.0 billion in 1967. Because this budget category also includes the entire social security system (old age, survivors, disability insurance, Medicare, and unemployment compensation), the proportion of total outlays disbursed via the states came to "only" 18 per cent for the year. The budget categories related to the national security showed, of course, an entirely different picture. Of total national defense outlays of slightly over $70 billion in 1967, not quite $27 million was disbursed in the form of grants-in-aid, mainly for civil defense programs. The international programs reported grants to states and their subdivisions totaling $6.5 million out of a budget of $4.1 billion. The civilian space program has not used the grant-in-aid device, at least up to the present time.

The growth of federal involvement in the domestic welfare programs has had an inevitable impact on the states, as the latter have become more dependent on the federal government for the provision of a major share of their revenue growth. Many functions, notably welfare, transportation, and education, which historically have been a local or private responsibility, are becoming subjects of national concern and federal decision-making, especially via the grant-in-aid mechanism. The states, in a sense, are becoming retail distributors of funds that the federal Treasury disburses in a more wholesale fashion.

Since the end of World War II, federal grants-in-aid to state and local governments have risen rapidly, both in absolute terms and in relation to state and local budgets. In 1946, federal grants totaled $900 million and were equal to 6 per cent of total state and local expenditures in that year. By 1967, these federal aid outlays had risen to $15 billion or 17 per cent of the combined expenditures of the states and their localities. The federal budget for the fiscal year 1969 projects a further growth of one-third in the total amount of federal grants-in-aid over 1967 to $20 billion.[1]

During the early part of the post-World War II period, traditional welfare programs—public assistance payments—constituted the largest area of support. The Federal-Aid Highway Act of 1954 resulted in a massive increase in federal grants in that historic era. The 1960's have seen rapid development, first of grants to education and, more recently, of grants directed at solving basic and general urban problems, especially reducing poverty and improving the living environment.

The Strings Attached to Federal Grants

Although the standard dictionary definition of *grant* is akin to that of gift, in practice federal grants are hardly in the nature of unrestricted bequests of federal largesse; they are "tied" or "conditional" grants rather than pure gifts.

The typical federal grant program imposes three requirements on the recipients: (1) that they devote the federal funds to specified purposes, (2) that they match the federal funds with their own resources, and (3) that the federal supervising agency approve in advance the detailed operating plans of the programs for which both the federal money and the state or local matching funds will be spent. Thus, the federal leverage on state and local budgets becomes substantial. Already, these federal grants produce three times as much revenue for states and localities as individual income taxes and five times as much as corporate income taxes.

A number of studies have shown that federal grants have a distorting effect on the expenditure patterns of the recipients.[2] This, of course, is hardly surprising. A fifty-fifty matching grant for public libraries, for example, would reduce the local price of a $1 million building to $500,000. Assuming some increase in demand in response to such a price reduction, the result is almost inevitable—the states spend more of their own funds on libraries and less on museums, parks, and other unaided functions than would otherwise be the case.

The extent of federal control and influence over state and local budgets is not immediately apparent in any dramatic fashion. One indication, of course, is the growing share of state-local expenditures that is financed by federal program grant funds. (From 12 per cent in 1958 to 17 per cent in 1967.)

Yet another important indication is the growth in matching funds which the states must put up in order to obtain the government money. In 1966, state and local governments had to provide a minimum of $5-$5.5 billion of their own funds in order to receive the $13 billion of federal grants disbursed that year. This means that, on the average, the recipients must raise close to $1.00 for every $2.00 forthcoming from the federal government (or in the aggregate about 7–8 per cent of general expenditure out of their own revenue sources). The ratio varies by major function, ranging from one-fourth of total program costs in many areas to one-half in natural resources. In 1969, based on the federal budget, required matching funds will rise to an estimated range of $8.5–$9.75 billion.[3] This gives the federal departments overseeing the grant programs a substantial measure of influence or control over those portions of the states' own budgets which are devoted to "matching" the federal grants.

Even more basic is the power of the federal departments to require their advance approval of state *operating* as well as *expenditure* plans before disbursing the grant money. For example, the federal-wide civil rights provision extends to all grant programs. As Title V of the Civil Rights Act of 1964 states, "No person in the United States shall, on the ground of race, color, or national origin, be excluded from participation in, be denied the benefits of, or be subjected to discrimination under any program or activity receiving federal financial assistance."[4]

Many of the grants stimulated by the Depression of the 1930's, particularly those authorized by the Social Security Act of 1935, provided for extensive supervision by the federal government. The national supervision includes the requirement that state and local personnel participating in federally aided programs of health, welfare, and employment be selected and administered under a civil service merit system.[5]

An examination of more recent federal grant-in-aid programs reveals many opportunities for the exercise of federal control or influence over state government budget and program decisions. For example, the U.S. Commissioner of Education must approve state plans for strengthening instruction in science and mathematics before the state education departments can receive federal aid funds for these programs. The Public Health Service approval of the state plan for cancer control is required before the federal grants are forthcoming. The Administration on Aging of HEW reviews state plans for community services for the aged prior to approving the federal grants. Further examples are abundant.

The Fiscal Mismatch

Pressures for further delegation of federal functions continue to mount. An increasingly popular justification for channeling federal funds through states and localities is what Walter Heller has termed "the fiscal mismatch."[6] This refers to the striking contrast between the federal budget outlook and state-local fiscal potentials.

For a considerable period of time, students of public finance have been impressed by the tendency of the federal government revenues to rise faster than the GNP, or even (during a cold war period) the expenditure requirements for existing programs. Essentially, this situation comes about because of two factors.

The first is the primary reliance by the federal government on an income tax with a generally progressive rate structure. By definition, the tax payment rises faster than the taxpayer's income under a progressive revenue structure. As a result, during periods of economic growth, the receipts from the federal tax structure, which is generally progressive, rise at a more rapid rate than the national income or the GNP.

The second factor is the dominant role of military programs in federal spending (about 42 per cent of the budget in the fiscal year 1965 and 43 per cent in 1969).[7] During periods of peace-time or even cold war, defense spending is relatively stable. Between 1956 and 1965—that is, during the decade between the Korean and Vietnam wars—national security purchases of goods and services rose by 25 per cent; however, the price index for federal purchases at the same time rose 27 per cent.[8] Hence, in real terms (adjusting for the effects of inflation) it can be seen that military spending was generally stable during a substantial period of cold war.

As a consequence, during periods short of hot war, total federal expenditures for existing federal programs (defense and nondefense combined) do not tend to rise as fast as the yield of the progressive tax structure. Individual civilian programs may be growing at a rapid rate but this effect is, by and large, offset by the virtual stability in the larger military share of the budget. Of course, substantial federal surpluses do not result. Under these conditions, the federal government is using the growing revenue potential to continually expand civilian programs, add new ones, and occasionally reduce tax rates.

Thus, the projected gap between federal revenues computed on the basis of existing tax laws and federal expenditures estimated on the basis of continuation of current programs mainly signifies the amount of discretion that may be exercised in the future. In retrospect, experience indicates that it is most unlikely that an entire decade will go by without important changes in either tax legislation or governmental program authorizations —most of which tend to eliminate the potential budget surplus.

Virtually every examination of state and local budgets reveals a very different relationship among revenues, expenditures, and economic growth. Unlike the federal government, the bulk of state and local revenues is obtained from regressive or proportional taxes (primarily on property and retail sales), and these are generally estimated to yield revenue increases at rates equal to or less than the growth in the GNP. At the same time, the requirements for existing state and local expenditure programs, notably education and welfare, tend to rise more rapidly than either the revenues from existing tax rates or the GNP. Thus, the Advisory Commission on Intergovernmental Relations has pointed out that in recent years state and local government spending has been rising at the rate of 8–9 per cent a year, or faster than the growth in the GNP. The commission believes that expenditures will continue to increase at this rate at least for some time, as long as the same forces that produced it continue to operate and additional ones develop.[9]

The fiscal outlook for state and local governments thus tends to be one of "potential" deficits. Hence, many observers suggest reallocating public resources so that a greater portion of federal revenues becomes available to assist state and local governments.

Alternatives to Tied or Conditional Grants

Because of the drawbacks of the existing grant-in-aid system, particularly the resulting federal control over state operations, many suggestions have been made for providing more unrestricted resources to state and local governments.

The general concept of federal distribution of general-aid funds to the states goes back to early American history. President Thomas Jefferson, in his second inaugural address, suggested a general program of federal aid to the states, to be used for such purposes as "rivers, canals, roads, arts, manufactures, education, and other great objects within each state." The lag between presidential recommendation and congressional action was quite considerable even then. It was not until 1837 (after the all-time record of twelve consecutive budget surpluses) that Congress did vote to distribute surplus funds. It did so on an approximately per capita basis. The $37 million so allocated was more than double the annual budget in those days.

The variety of uses to which the states devoted these windfall revenues is intriguing. Some used the funds to capitalize the state banks; others devoted the money to local debt repayment or public works. Some objected to the whole idea. The Georgia legislature stated that they would have refused the money had it not been for the provision that the share of any refusing state would be divided among the other states. Although, according to one scholarly observer, some of the funds were "lost" or "wasted on improvements," the major portion was utilized for education and other undefined "worthy purposes."[10]

Historians argue over the economic effects of the distribution of idle federal funds to the states. In any event, the payments were halted when they were three-quarters completed. The Panic of 1837 had turned the federal budget surpluses into a deficit. This "unique and curious measure," to use the terms of one historian, was allowed to lapse.[11] Considerable interest in the general distribution of federal funds to the states arose again in the 1880's, but did not result in any federal action.

Under the Eisenhower administration, an effort was made to return the vocational education program and the construction of waste treatment facilities (which had been supported by federal grants) to full state financial control and responsibility. This did not arouse much state interest, and failed to be enacted even though it contained a sweetener—a portion of the federal excise on local telephone service was to be yielded to the states (the revenues at the time exceeded the costs of the programs to be transferred).

More recently, efforts have been made to move from very specific grants which control state or local programs in great detail to broader ones covering general categories such as health, education, or welfare. Thus far, these efforts also have been unsuccessful.

More basic changes are envisioned in the various programs for sharing a portion of the yield of the federal income taxes with states and/or local governments. Prior to the Vietnam War there was considerable public discussion of the fiscal dividend which was going to be brought about by the combination of a rapidly growing economy and a progressive federal income tax. Support began to grow for a fairly novel use of the growth in federal revenues, above the built-in cost increases of ongoing federal programs—block grants to the states, that is, financial aid with no strings attached, or at least not many.

Although Democratic economists like Walter Heller, former chairman of the CEA, publicized the idea,[12] Republicans like the Congressmen Melvin Laird,[13] Howard Baker, Charles Goodell, and Jacob K. Javits introduced bills and tried to put the concept into practice. Under various labels, tax sharing or block grants seemed to become a bipartisan concern.

Then came the Vietnam War and the dreams of a fiscal dividend turned into the reality of massive budget deficits. Thus, reallocating "surplus" federal resources to the states and cities was deferred to the post-Vietnam agenda. What priority is to be assigned that particular use of federal revenues remains unresolved. In part that may depend on the evaluation by the public and Congress of the attractiveness of the states as an instrumentality for dealing with such difficult problems as reducing poverty, improving urban transportation, combating environmental pollution, rebuilding ghetto housing, upgrading education and training for minority groups, and so forth.

As we have seen, the competitors for federal funds and national attention are numerous. Private corporations oriented to meeting the needs and requirements of the federal government offer an array of sophisticated services, ranging from operating Job Corps camps to designing urban transportation systems and retraining the unemployed. Nonprofit institutions are running regional education laboratories, conducting anti-poverty programs, and offering to do research and development work on virtually every national ill. Within the public sector itself, federal agencies and local governments all represent alternative mechanisms for dealing with nationwide problems.

Reallocating federal revenues to the states would help to restore greater fiscal balance to our federal form of government. It could also help to redress the cumulative bypassing of the states that we have witnessed in the formation of new public programs—the war on poverty, mass transportation, housing, and so forth. This approach would appear to constitute an important step toward achieving what President Richard Nixon envisioned during the 1968 election campaign as "a streamlined Federal system, with a return to the states, cities, and communities of the decision-making power rightfully theirs."

However, this approach may only succeed in obtaining the necessary public support if the states can succeed in convincing the people that it truly represents state assumption of responsibility as well as of funds—that in choosing the mechanisms for conducting the public business and achieving major natural objectives, the nation would be wise to give the states a larger role than at present.

Meanwhile, the states and localities attempt to limp along in dealing with the current array of revenue sources and program responsibilities. In practice, of course, the actual state and local deficits are narrowed or eliminated by a variety of discretionary actions. Tax rates are continually raised; new tax sources are introduced; property assessment ratios are increased; desirable programs are deferred or cut back; and of course federal grants-in-aid are more heavily relied upon.

Numerous detailed proposals to correct the "fiscal mismatch" have been made. Many of these alternatives would make fundamental changes in the status quo. Some would lessen substantially the tendency for state and local governments to become agents of the federal departments conducting federally approved programs with federal funds. Rather, many of them would give the states relatively complete discretion over the use of these funds. Conversely, some of the new approaches would bypass state and local governments entirely. Inevitably, almost every one of these alternatives has some undesirable effects which may or may not be present in the existing grant system. All of the alternatives that are analyzed below possess a common characteristic: they would ease the financial pressures on state and local governments, although to varying degrees and in different ways.

Alternative Methods of Federal Aid

A variety of alternative methods has been suggested whereby the federal government can reduce the financial pressures on state and local governments. These vary from traditional solutions—such as more categorical grants-in-aid or additional federal assumption of program responsibilities—to more innovative approaches, such as block grants or tax sharing which would increase state and local discretion over how they spend the funds available to them.[14]

Table 5–1 is an attempt to classify the major types of proposals that have been made from the viewpoint of their impact on the federal system (the major alternatives are analyzed in more detail below).

TABLE 5–1 *Alternative Types of Federal Aid to State and Local Governments*

	Traditional	Innovative
Relatively conservative	Federal tax reductions, which tend to reduce size of federal sector and make more private funds available for state and local taxation.	Tax credits, which may soften taxpayer resistance to state and local taxation, but provide no funds directly. Also tax sharing, which allocates funds according to source of federal revenue collections (emphasis on wealthier states).
Relatively liberal	Larger direct federal programs, which may reduce pressures on the states and localities.	Block grants with many strings especially providing heavy emphasis on low-income regions and large cities and limited to health-education welfare.
Mixed solutions	Various methods which do not increase state or local discretion—using business firms, nonprofits, etc., to conduct federal programs; more categorical grants; additional transfer payments, including a negative income tax.	Revenue sharing with few strings—lump sum payment to state and local governments on a per capita basis or close to it.

TAX SHARING Under tax-sharing plans, a fixed portion of federal personal income-tax revenues would be distributed to each state in proportion to the amount of federal taxes which were paid by the citizens of the state. The state governments would be left free to determine the uses to which they wish to put the funds they receive. Tax sharing would give the states a vested interest in the current high rates of federal income taxation; in fact, we would expect the states to oppose any actions which would reduce the yield of the federal income tax and to favor legislation to raise rates, reduce exemptions, close loopholes, and so forth.

The federal government historically has shared with the states revenues from a few small tax sources. These include sharing internal revenue collections with the Virgin Islands, sharing customs receipts with Puerto Rico and the Virgin Islands, and sharing a variety of natural resource-type receipts with the states in which these resources (land, wildlife, and power) are located.

TAX CREDITS The federal tax structure currently provides credits for two types of state taxes: a limited credit for state death taxes against federal estate-tax liabilities, and a 90 per cent credit against federal payroll levies for similar payments into state unemployment compensation systems.

A general tax credit—such as the proposal to credit 40 per cent of state income-tax payments towards federal personal income taxes due, as recommended by the Advisory Commission on Intergovernmental Relations—differs from tax sharing in two main ways. No federal funds would go directly to state or local governments, but federal revenues would be reduced. The imposition, collection, and use of the state income tax is left in the hands of the state governments. Hence, they would only benefit to the extent that the federal credit softens taxpayer resistance and thus enables the states to institute or raise income taxes above the levels otherwise politically acceptable.

From the viewpoint of the individual taxpayer, a tax credit

would result in a lower federal tax bill by giving him a more generous write-off of state taxes. It would offer an option of either deducting his state-tax payments from taxable income, as he can do now, or to deduct a stipulated fraction of his state-tax payments from his federal tax bill.

The major benefit would accrue to persons in the low- and middle-income brackets. Persons in the higher tax brackets (above 40 per cent in the case of a 40 per cent credit) already enjoy a more liberal write-off through itemization. The tax credit proposal analyzed here is that which Professor James Maxwell examined in a study for the Brookings Institution.[15]

EXPANSION OF PROGRAMS CARRIED ON AT THE FEDERAL LEVEL Potential increases in federal revenue, over and above those required for financing continuing programs, could be assigned to new or expanded domestic civilian operations which the federal government would carry on in each of the fifty states. Examples of such new programs of an interstate character could include the construction and operation of mass transportation or the guaranteed annual-income schemes discussed in the previous chapter. Alternatively, the national government could increase the volume of funding for existing federal programs, such as public works in the fields of electric power, irrigation, and recreation.

These direct federal programs would result in the largest amount of direct federal intervention in the economy of any of the policy alternatives examined here, since there would be no state or local government participation. To some extent, there would be state and local benefits, since facilities or services would be provided which otherwise might not be available or would have to be financed locally.

For purposes of analysis, direct federal operations in the comparisons below are measured by the wages and salaries of federal civilian employees; data on geographical distribution of wage and salary payments are of good statistical quality and readily available.[16]

FEDERAL GRANTS LIMITED TO SPECIFIC PROGRAM AREAS As an alternative to direct operations of its own, the federal government could increase the volume and number of conditional or program grants to state and local governments. This traditional type of federal aid is limited to very specific functions, such as "strengthening instruction in the humanities and the arts" or "heart disease control," where, as we have seen, the federal agency administering the program sets detailed standards for the approval of individual state and local projects. As of January 1966, there were 300 separate authorizations for federal assistance to state and local governments, covering 162 major programs.[17] It is often a fine line between setting national standards and exercising strong federal control.

This alternative would avoid direct federal operation of the public activities to be financed. However, it would increase further the impact of federal decision-making on state and local policies and practices.

Most federal grants are awarded directly to state governments, yet significant precedents exist for the national government's bypassing the states and dealing directly with localities. Examples of such grant programs include housing and urban renewal, federal aid to airports, and aid to mass transportation systems. In the aggregate, $9.9 billion of federal aid payments were made to the states in the fiscal year 1965, and $1.2 billion directly to local units.

STRAIGHT BLOCK GRANTS Block grants—not limited to specific program areas—have been widely utilized in other nations, notably Great Britain and Canada. The basic concept of block grants is to make the federal aid to the states completely unconditional. The most straightforward method of distribution would be on a per capita basis. One approach is to set up a permanent trust fund to distribute a fixed portion of the federal income-tax base among the states each year regardless of the level of program grants or the state of the federal budget. In effect, a major portion of the growth in federal revenues would be disbursed to the states; revenue available for direct federal operations would continue to grow at a rapid rate, but the absolute amounts would be lower than otherwise.

Some observers maintain that unlike the other suggested forms of federal aid, block grants would go to the root of the fiscal dilemma plaguing state and local governments. This method would provide a revenue source that would grow rapidly as the national economy expands and incomes rise. It would help free states from the compulsion to look over their shoulders at what adjacent states are doing to attract industry before undertaking their own spending programs. Also, long-term planning by states and localities would be facilitated since the regular flow of funds would eliminate the uncertainties which are characteristic of the annual appropriations process. A major criticism, however, is that block grants would divorce the responsibility for collecting taxes from decisions on their use.

BLOCK GRANTS WITH EQUALIZATION   Most of the block grant bills introduced in Congress contain some departures from a straight per capita distribution, the most universal being an equalization feature. The bill that has received perhaps the most attention was introduced by Senator Jacob K. Javits of New York and cosponsored by Senators Vance Hartke of Indiana, Hugh Scott of Pennsylvania, and Karl E. Mundt of South Dakota.[18] It provides for annual block grants equal to 1 per cent of the total taxable personal income. Under present conditions, this would amount to about $3 billion a year and would increase as the tax base expands.

Like almost every specific proposal that has been introduced, the Javits Plan is somewhat more restrictive than the original block grant concept. The funds could only be used in the broad categories of health, education, and welfare. Also, states with low tax efforts would be penalized and those with high tax efforts rewarded. Tax effort (the total yield of state and local taxes as a percentage of aggregate personal income in the state) is a standard measure of the extent to which state and local governments are using their own resources to solve public problems. This concept adjusts for the fact that some poor states do not raise large amounts of revenue even though they try harder than average (Mississippi and Alabama traditionally report high tax efforts but, because of the low income base, their tax yields are low).

Thus, a state whose tax effort is 10 per cent above the national average might have its basic amount of federal block grant funds increased by 10 per cent; a state whose tax effort is 10 per cent below would experience a proportional reduction.

A related suggestion is to lower the share of any state which reduces its tax revenues from the current level. The intent would be to discourage states from using the federal money to reduce their own tax rates.

Payments would be made under the following formula: (1) 80 per cent would be distributed on the basis of population, and would be increased or decreased depending on the state's own tax effort as compared with the national average; and (2) 20 per cent would be paid to the thirteen states with the lowest per capita income, and would be distributed according to the population of the states involved.

The states, in turn, would be required to distribute an "equitable" portion of their allotments to local governments, which must be at least the average of the distribution of their own revenues to local governments over the previous five years.

Comparisons among the Alternatives

A major theme underlying many of the proposals for federal aid to state and local governments is the desirability of reducing the inequality of incomes among the various states and regions of the United States. This would particularly enable the poorer areas to support a higher level of public services, more nearly approximating that of the nation as a whole. The externalities often accompanying state and local government activities—benefits enjoyed by those outside of the taxing jurisdiction—are cited as a crucial reason for enabling the poorer states to provide a higher level of services than they could finance from their own resources. Such externalities arise, for example, when persons reared and educated in one region move to and produce income in another.

TABLE 5–2 *State Shares of Federal Aid Alternatives*

State Grouping	Tax Sharing	Tax Credits	Direct Federal Programs	Existing Program Grants	Per Capita Block Grants	Block Grants with Equalization
17 states with highest per capita incomes*	66%	61%	57%	46%	50%	39%
17 middle-income states	20	23	23	25	25	20
17 states with lowest per capita incomes	14	16	20	29	25	41
TOTAL	100	100	100	100	100	100

* Sixteen states and the District of Columbia.
SOURCE: Murray L. Weidenbaum, "Federal Aid to State and Local Governments: The Policy Alternatives," in U.S. Congress, Joint Economic Committee, *Revenue Sharing and Its Alternatives* (Washington, D.C.: U.S. Government Printing Office, 1967), XI, 651–665.

Table 5–2 contains a summary analysis of the state shares of the six alternative aid proposals considered in this study. It is apparent that block grants with equalization (such as provided by the Javits bill) would channel far more funds into the low-income areas than any of the other alternatives; hence, they are the most income-equalizing in a geographic sense. It is also interesting to note that existing federal program grants to state and local government are more income-equalizing than would be block grants distributed on a simple per capita basis.[19] It also can be seen that direct federal programs, as measured by the wages and salaries of civilian government employees, do not particularly favor low-income areas. (Federal employment tends to be concentrated in the population centers of the more industrialized and hence higher income states.) As would be expected, tax credits and tax sharing provide the smallest amounts to low-income areas. Of course, the reverse rank order holds when the shares of the high-income states are examined.[20]

EFFECT ON LOCAL GOVERNMENTS One of the major questions concerning the distribution of federal funds without strings—via the tax sharing, tax credit, and per capita block grant approaches —is the extent to which the states will "pass through" some of the funds to local government units. The concern on the part of the cities, which traditionally believe that they receive less than "fair" shares from the state legislatures, is evidenced by proposals that they have made for block grants directly from the federal government, which would completely bypass the states.

It is the rare state government that convincingly shows that it is truly interested in the problems of its urban citizens, particularly the urban poor. One indication of the nonurban orientation of state governments is so obvious that it is taken for granted or overlooked. Where are the state capitals located, and hence, where do legislators meet to carry on the state's business, and where do so many of the administrators of state programs live and work? We find the capitals of many of our largest states, some of those with the heaviest concentration of urban-racial-poverty problems, to be relatively small- or medium-sized cities, facing in a sense a different set of problems and concerns.

An examination of the list of these major state capitals is instructive: New York—Albany; Illinois—Springfield; Pennsylvania —Harrisburg; New Jersey—Trenton; Missouri—Jefferson City; Texas—Austin; and Wisconsin—Madison. These cities certainly are not insignificant townships. Yet neither are they the metropolises of one million or more which have been featured so prominently in the news of serious unrest.

Only five out of the fifty state capitals are located in a metropolitan area with a population of one million or more. In contrast, almost two-fifths of the nation's total population now lives in these metropolises. If the states are to continue as the mainstay of our federal system, they will have to overcome their inability or unwillingness to face up to the major domestic problems in a meaningful way. Otherwise, the result could be a fundamental weakening of our federal form of government.

Many of the revenue-sharing bills introduced in Congress do have a "pass through" provision. Most of these would penalize states that give local governments a smaller share of the federal funds than they receive of state money. Some observers contend that this would merely maintain past and current inequities. The supporters of block grants count heavily on reapportionment for redressing the balance. It would appear that the city-state relationship approaches one of rivalry rather than the image of close cooperation that often underlies the formation of public policies with reference to state governments.

Perhaps a more equitable method of state sharing with local units is the suggestion that the amount of funds "passed through" be based on the proportion of locally raised revenues to total state and local revenues; on the average, localities raised 50 per cent of combined state and local general revenues in 1967.

The "pass through" arrangement in a sense is a compromise between those who would give the states complete discretion and those who would have a large portion of the so-called federal revenue sharing funds go directly from the federal Treasury to individual local governments.

The Hard Choices Ahead

As might be expected, the foregoing analysis does not come up with a clear-cut answer as to which single federal aid approach is most desirable or likely to be enacted. Any of the newer approaches (block grants or tax sharing or tax credits) would cause important changes in the status quo, but the changes would differ. Block grants may be more "income-equalizing," at least in a geographic sense, but they do have some strings attached which limit the freedom of action of the state governments. Tax sharing would come with no strings, but it would channel a disproportionately large share of the funds to the wealthiest states. In contrast, tax credits would influence state legislatures to depend more heavily on one particular type of taxation (the income tax), thus to some extent reducing their fiscal sovereignty. In contrast, increasing reliance on direct federal operations would reduce the financial pressures on the states, but in a sense help to put them out of business for lack of both resources and program responsibility. All of the measures designed to provide financial aid to the states share a common characteristic: they transfer purchasing power from the federal government to the states.

In some cases, the plans also would provide aid to the cities. However, many of the bills being considered would leave to the states the task of dividing the federal funds with the cities, counties, and other local subdivisions. Judging by current conditions, it is not likely that the states would voluntarily turn over a major share of the federal funds to the cities for use in meeting the urgent and interrelated racial-poverty-urban problems. Thus, no single financial mechanism seems likely to meet all of the major emerging public policy needs of the nation.

One reasonable approach might be for the federal government to consolidate the many hundreds of grant-in-aid programs it now conducts into about a dozen, covering each of the major substantive areas (transportation, health, education, income maintenance, and so forth). This act alone would tend to reduce administrative costs and increase the freedom of action of state governments.

Looking forward, increases in federal revenue that follow the end of the Vietnam War should in good part be funneled to state and local governments via block grants. These fiscal aids should only have a few basic strings: mandatory sharing by the states with local governments based on the existing allocation of functions in each state between state and local activities; an equalization provision favoring the poorest states; a tax effort factor encouraging state and local governments to rely more on their own resources; and already required civil rights protection. The allocation of the funds by program area should be left to the spending unit, thus helping to bring some aspects of government activity as close to the grass roots level as possible. Hence, a general program of revenue sharing could help achieve simultaneously the fiscal objective of reducing the financial pressures on state and local governments and the administrative objective of greater decentralization of governmental decision-making.

A Recapitulation

There undoubtedly will remain important areas of natural concern with which the federal government will wish to deal directly. Here, the array of private mechanisms can be drawn upon—government-oriented corporations, commercially oriented enterprises, nonprofit institutions set up at federal instance, more independently established private nonprofit organizations, and perhaps some joint ventures and new combinations of these institutional approaches.

Certainly the federal sector dealing through private intermediaries constitutes an alternative to increasing reliance on state and local governments through program or block grants. However, as we have seen, contracts with and grants to private organizations—either business firms or nonprofit groups—also generate adverse side effects as well as the more obvious benefits. Hence, hard choices will continue to face governmental policymakers who will be dealing with the ever-changing array of challenges, pressures, and responsibilities facing the federal government.

Perhaps these responses will continue to take a variety of institutional forms, involving state and local governments, business firms, and nonprofit organizations in different ways as the various individual government programs develop. Table 5-3 shows the variety of mechanisms currently used in the larger functions of the federal government. As Somers and Somers point out, "Our political and social structure demands a high degree of pluralism."[21] The trend for greater federal delegation and contracting

TABLE 5-3 *The Variety of Mechanisms Used in Federal Programs*
(Mechanism Utilized)

Major Domestic Function	Government-Oriented Corporations	Grants to State, Local Governments	Intergovernmental Agencies	Quasi-Private Institutions	Fiscal Intermediaries	Direct Federal Operations
Health, labor and welfare		Public assistance, health, manpower	Regional pollution control agencies	Poverty organizations	Medicare	Maritime health facilities
Education		Aid to school districts	Regional education planning agencies	Educational laboratories		Smithsonian Institution
Housing		Traditional urban renewal		Ghetto rebuilding		
Commerce and transportation	Supersonic transport	Highways, airports	Regional development commissions	Comsat, Federal Reserve System		FAA facilities
Agriculture		A & M Colleges	Regional marketing boards	Local farm committees, federal land banks		
Veterans						VA hospitals
General government						Public buildings
National defense	Weapon systems					Armed Services
Space	Space vehicles					NASA laboratories

out of functions and programs—especially the newer ones—appears to be a strong and growing one in governmental affairs in the United States.

NOTES

1. "Federal Aid to State and Local Governments," *Special Analyses, Budget of the United States, Fiscal Year 1969* (Washington, D.C.: U.S. Government Printing Office, 1968), pp. 155–174 (hereafter referred to as *Special Analysis of the Budget*).

2. Governmental Affairs Institute, *Impact of Federal Grants-in-Aid on South Carolina,* A Report to the Commission on Intergovernmental Relations (Washington, D.C., 1954); McKinsey and Company, *The Impact of Federal Grants-in-Aid in the State of Washington* (San Francisco, 1954).

3. *Special Analysis of the Budget,* p. 162.

4. Cited on the inside cover of U.S. Department of Health, Education, and Welfare, *Grants-in-Aid and Other Financial Assistance Programs Administered by the U.S. Department of Health, Education, and Welfare* (Washington, D.C.: U.S. Government Printing Office, 1967).

5. U.S. Congress, Senate, *Periodic Congressional Reassessments of Federal Grants-in-Aid to State and Local Governments,* prepared by the Advisory Commission on Intergovernmental Relations for the Committee on Government Operations, 90th Cong., 1st Sess., pp. 2–3.

6. Walter W. Heller, "The Future of Our Fiscal System," *Journal of Business,* XXXVIII, No. 3 (July 1965), 240.

7. U.S. Bureau of the Budget, *The Budget of the United States Government, Fiscal Year 1969* (Washington, D.C.: U.S. Government Printing Office, 1968), p. 540.

8. *Economic Report of the President, January 1967* (Washington, D.C.: U. S. Government Printing Office, 1967), pp. 213, 217.

9. Advisory Commission on Intergovernmental Relations, *Federal-State Coordination of Personal Income Taxes* (Washington, D.C.: U.S. Government Printing Office, October 1965), p. 3.

10. Edward G. Bourne, *The History of the Surplus Revenue of 1837* (New York: G. P. Putnam's Sons, 1885).

11. Bray Hammond, *Banks and Politics in America: From the Revo-

lution to the Civil War (Princeton: Princeton University Press, 1957), p. 45.

12. Walter W. Heller, *New Dimensions of Political Economy* (New York: W. W. Norton & Company, 1967), pp. 139–155.

13. Representative Melvin R. Laird, "Strengthening the Federal System—The Case for Revenue Sharing," *Congressional Record* (February 15, 1967), pp. 1330–49; Senator Howard Baker, "Introduction of Tax Sharing Act of 1969," *Congressional Record* (March 24, 1969), pp. 53131–53134; Jacob Javits, "Federal-State Tax-Sharing Plan," *Congressional Record* (October 11, 1965), pp. 25608–25619.

14. This analysis draws upon the author's earlier work, "Federal Aid to State and Local Governments; The Policy Alternatives," in U.S. Congress, Joint Economic Committee, *Revenue Sharing and Its Alternatives: What Future for Fiscal Federalism?* Vol. II (Washington, D.C.: U.S. Government Printing Office, 1967).

15. His data cover a credit for state income taxes of 7 per cent of federal individual income-tax liability in 1958. *Cf.* James A. Maxwell, *Tax Credits and Intergovernmental Fiscal Relations* (Washington, D.C.: Brookings Institution, 1962), pp. 184–185.

16. The data used were taken from *Survey of Current Business,* August 1964, pp. 18–21.

17. I. M. Labovitz, *Number of Authorizations for Federal Assistance to State and Local Governments under Laws in Force at Selected Dates During 1964–66* (Washington, D.C.: Library of Congress, July 5, 1966).

18. *Congressional Record* (October 11, 1965), pp. 25616–25617.

19. The basic data on the distribution of federal grants to the states are taken from *Annual Report of the Secretary of the Treasury on the State of the Finances for the Fiscal Year 1964* (Washington, D.C.: U.S. Government Printing Office, 1966), p. 11.

20. The basic data on federal tax collections are taken from *1964 Annual Report, Commissioner of Internal Revenue* (Washington, D.C.: U.S. Government Printing Office, 1965), p. 73.

21. Herman M. Somers and Anne R. Somers, *Medicare and the Hospitals: Issues and Prospects* (Washington, D.C.: Brookings Institution, 1967), p. 272.

6

MACROECONOMIC IMPACTS: THE NEW
PUBLIC SECTOR AND FISCAL POLICY

The first five chapters of this book have been discussing various
aspects of the public sector of the United States. Yet, no definition of the public sector has been presented. Actually, this is
common practice in most discussions of the public sector, and
there are some good reasons for this. First of all, definitions in
general are usually tedious affairs. Second, and of greater importance here, a technically accurate definition in this case is not
likely to correspond to the general understanding of the term.
Nevertheless, making a few distinctions is necessary to advance
our understanding of the role of the modern public sector.

In theory, the public sector only comprises the value of the
output produced by government employees. However, there is
no market for government products—they are generally given
away to the public, which finances general government operations through taxes and investment in the national debt. Hence,
there is no mechanism for directly quantifying, particularly in
dollar terms, the output resulting from government activities.

Conventionally, economists resort to measuring this public
output indirectly, by the price of the inputs—which are primarily
the payments to government employees. On this basis, the federal

portion of the public sector of the United States (that is, the wages and salaries paid to federal employees) came to $33 billion in 1966. The federal sector thus came to only 4 per cent of the GNP of $743 billion for the year.[1] This measure of the federal sector is important, because it indicates that only a small share of the nation's output (4 per cent) is actually produced by the federal government; the remaining 96 per cent of the GNP represents primarily private production (90 per cent) and a relatively small amount of state and local government output (6 per cent). Hence, the actual degree of socialization of the American economy borders on the minute.

In more common practice, however, economists include in their definition of the public sector not only the wages and salaries of government employees, but the purchases of goods and services that government agencies make from the private sector. The rationale is that the governmentally procured items are not available for private use. Such federal procurement came to 6 per cent of the GNP in 1966. When we add the "output" of the government's own employees to its purchases we arrive at the figure of 10 per cent as the total share of the GNP allocated directly to the federal government.

Yet, that is not the whole story. Because of the intertwining of the public and private sectors that we have noted earlier, the expenditures and activities of the federal government show up in many parts of the economy. The production of goods and services for the federal agencies by the government-oriented corporations at times can have important impacts in the business (or, technically, investment) sector. The quasi-governmental organizations have an unexpected effect on private consumption expenditures. Finally, as would be expected, grants-in-aid influence state and local government purchases.

It is interesting to note that the first round impact of federal activities on the GNP shows up in all sectors of the economy—personal consumption expenditures, gross private domestic investment, net exports, and government purchases. Some of the items may be obvious and others require a bit more explanation.

Personal Consumption Expenditures

Perhaps the oddest aspect of governmental involvement in the private sector arises from the fact that the outlays of all private nonprofit organizations are included along with consumer purchases of goods and services in the GNP subcategory of "personal consumption expenditures."[2] Hence, federal grants to the regional educational laboratories and to the anti-poverty community action organizations show up as they are respent by the recipients in this apparently quite nongovernmental category. In 1966, $689 million of the purchases by private nonprofit institutions were funded by federal grants and contracts. The estimate for 1967 is $800 million and this item is likely to continue rising rapidly.[3]

Also, but not unexpectedly, governmental transfer payments (for example, veterans' pensions and social security benefits) generally become personal consumption expenditures as the proceeds are spent by the recipients. Such transfer-payment programs themselves do not use up real resources and hence do not reduce the amount available for private disposition. They do change the availability of these resources to different groups in society. For example, the social security program (including both social security taxes and benefit payments) takes resources from the younger members of the community and increases the resources available to the elderly without necessarily changing the total amount of resources available to society.

Similarly, unemployment compensation transfers resources from the employed to the unemployed. In contrast, Medicare—although it transfers resources similarly to other transfer payments—possesses some of the market impact characteristic of government purchases. Medicare directly affects the allocation of resources by enabling the beneficiaries to increase their consumption of medical and health services. Indeed, that was a major purpose of the law, along with the desire to provide insurance to cover the high cost of illness in old age. It was designed to encourage and make possible a specific kind of resource use believed desirable by society, rather than simply to enhance the economic position of the elderly for whatever use they might desire to make of the added income.[4]

Gross Private Domestic Investment

In the case of large and technically complex items—which dominate military, space, and atomic energy procurement programs—business firms supplying these commodities to the government do not furnish them out of inventory but produce them "custom made," so to speak, on government order. Hence, there is generally an extended period of time between the beginning of production on a government order and the delivery of the end item by the private business contractor.

As noted in Chapter 2, because of the size of these orders and the length of the production period (the long "lead time" for designing and producing weapon systems is the term generally used), the federal government typically makes progress payments to the contractor during the production period. However, these progress payments are not recorded in the government sector. Because these progress payments are considered financing transactions, they do not show up anywhere in the GNP.

Hence, all through the production period for aircraft, missiles, space systems, and similar specialized durable goods ordered by federal agencies—while income is being earned by the labor and the other factors of production and while the government is making substantial part payments on the items it has ordered—the value of the output is being recorded not in the public sector but in the private sector (in the change in inventory portion of gross private domestic investment). Certainly, if the Department of Defense relied on its own arsenals rather than on contracts with private corporations, these involuted economic impacts involving the private sector as well as the public sector simply would not occur. They reflect yet another aspect of the delegating or contracting out of federal government activities.

As will be shown below, the failure to understand that the initial impact of government procurement activity shows up in the private sector rather than in the public sector was a key source of economic difficulty during the military buildup for the Vietnam War. This lack of economic understanding also could hamper effective policy for adjusting to a military cutback.

Net Exports of Goods and Services

Most of the foreign aid expenditures of the federal government are used for goods and services produced in the United States and shipped to other countries. The proportion manufactured in the United States was 82 per cent in the fiscal year 1966 and rose to 88 per cent in 1967.[5] However, these governmental disbursements are not recorded in the GNP as government purchases but in the private sector, as exports of goods and services. This is brought out quite clearly in the official description by the Office of Business Economics:

> Private exports include those goods transferred from the ownership of private United States residents to foreign ownership. In accordance with this definition, goods furnished under the European recovery program and other Government aid programs are considered to be private exports if the title passes direct from the United States supplier to the foreign recipient country. (The offsetting cash payment by the Economic Cooperation Administration [later the Mutual Security Agency] to the US supplier or to the foreign government would, however, be shown as a Government unilateral transfer.)[6]

A related item is the sales which the federal government makes overseas. These are primarily items of military equipment which are sold to the armed forces of other nations. In the national income accounts, such sales are deducted from federal government purchases and included in exports of goods and services.[7]

Sales of military equipment have been rising in recent years. In the fiscal year 1961, Department of Defense cash receipts from overseas operations were slightly over $300 million. By fiscal 1963 these sales were well above $1 billion and reached

$1.6 billion in the fiscal year 1967.[8] Again, these governmental exports are another indication—a generally overlooked one—of the role of the federal government in the American economy.

Government Purchases of Goods and Services

The 10 per cent of GNP devoted to federal purchases offers a rather clearly defined case of the role of the national government in the American economy. However, to this obvious segment there properly should be added—in order to fully gauge the federal economic impact—the purchases by state and local government which are financed by federal grants-in-aid and shared revenues. The payments to the states for highway construction, for example, channel and redirect to a specific purpose, certain uses of labor, materials, and machines—scarce resources which the nation might have used in some other way. These amounted to $11 billion in 1966.

The Combined Impact

Table 6–1 is an exploratory attempt to identify and quantify the federal role in each of the major sectors of the GNP. It can be seen that the federal government, on the basis of the approach used here, accounted for 13 per cent of the GNP in 1966. Of much greater long-run significance, however, is the point that as the federal government increases its utilization of mechanisms in other sectors of the economy, conventional measures become more and more inadequate. In 1966, total measurable direct federal involvement in GNP came to $98 billion, compared to the traditional measure—federal purchases of goods and services—which showed $77 billion. By 1970, the gap between the two measures is likely to have widened considerably, particularly if the end of the Vietnam War leads to a major national effort to deal with the urban-racial-poverty complex of difficult domestic problems.

However, the need to understand the full macroeconomic

impact of the public sector transcends mere attempts at better aggregate quantification. An indication of the importance of such an understanding is obtained when we examine the unfortunate results which have occurred during recent periods when the nation did not understand the way in which new government purchase programs work out their effects on the economy. Thus, the expansion in military demand accompanying both the Korean and Vietnam wars resulted in substantial inflationary pressures and led to other, even more serious political and economic con-

TABLE 6-1 *Measuring Federal Involvement in Economic Activity, 1966*

Sector of the Economy	Amount Recorded in GNP (billions)	Nature of Federal Involvement	Amount Federally Financed (billions)
Personal consumption expenditures	$466	Federal financing of nonprofit institutions	$1*
Gross private domestic investment	118	Increase in inventories of government contractors	5
Net exports of goods and services	5	U.S. foreign aid Military sales	2 2
Government purchases of goods and services:			
Federal	77	Total	77
State and local	77	Federal grants	11
TOTAL	743		98

* Excludes consumer spending financed by $30 billion of transfer payments from the federal government and $7 billion of state and local transfer payments funded through federal grants to state and local governments.

SOURCE: U.S. Departments of Commerce and Defense; budget documents.

sequences. As will be demonstrated below, a proper understanding of the role of the modern public sector in the American economy might have averted these results.

The Federal Government Spending Process

In order to detect the problems involved in measuring the economic impact of a military buildup, it is necessary to review the sequences of the process by which the federal government makes its expenditures.

As a starting point, we may take the Presidential budget which is transmitted to Congress each January and which covers the twelve-month period beginning the following July 1. The Presidential recommendations are subjected to many months of detailed congressional scrutiny and to numerous revisions before the funds are appropriated. Following quarterly apportionment of the funds by the Bureau of the Budget, the various federal agencies commit the funds appropriated to them for their various authorized activities. Thus the funds are "obligated." For many government programs, disbursements follow rather quickly. Pension payments to veterans, interest payments to holders of the national debt, and wage and salary payments to government employees are made when or very soon after funds are obligated.

However, obligations for major items of equipment purchased from the private sector are in the form of orders awarded or contracts placed; such transactions are not soon followed by an equivalent amount of government expenditure. Particularly in the case of military weapon systems, a considerable amount of time is necessary for the design, production, and delivery of the items ordered. The delays involved are hardly trivial. During the Korean War, the lag between ordering and delivering military items varied from six months for uniforms to fifteen months for tanks to over two years for combat aircraft. The "lead time" for procurement of ammunition for Vietnam has been estimated at six months, for aircraft, eighteen months.[9]

In the case of military procurement programs, it is clear that the placement of orders with defense contractors and their commencement or expansion of production generate demands for resources, which are evidenced by the hiring of manpower and the acquisition and utilization of materials. The key problem here, however, is that all such productive activity and its effect on income shows up in the private sector and not in the public sector.

The progress payments which the federal government makes to its contractors in the course of production are recorded in the federal budget at the time they are made. However, the GNP ignores such "financial" transactions and only takes account of the actual later delivery of the completed weapons. Only after the work is completed and incomes have already been earned by the factors of production are the items delivered to the government. The transaction is then recorded as a government purchase, but a corresponding and offsetting decline occurs in business inventories. Hence, the delivery stage has no impact on the GNP. The expansive effect of the government purchase on economic activity occurred earlier, following the receipt of the government order and the commencement of production. In practice, indirect effects may occur, such as anticipatory effects on consumer spending and business investment flowing from the announcement of the new or expanded government program or from the placement of large contracts. In general, however, these other effects reenforce the basic point that most of the economic impact occurs prior to the recording of government purchases in the GNP.

The Korean Experience

The Korean mobilization—as well as the Vietnam military buildup—posed just such problems of identifying the timing of the economic impact of government spending. Using conventional measures, federal fiscal policy during the period of the initial Korean buildup, the fiscal year 1951 (July 1, 1950–June 30, 1951) seemed appropriately restraining. Federal expenditures rose a modest 11 per cent and the overall budget showed a $3.5 billion surplus.[10]

However, a different story emerges from an examination of the statistical data used to measure the earlier stages of the government spending process. The amount of appropriations granted by Congress in the fiscal year 1951 was two-thirds again higher than the 1950 total. The aggregate amount of contracts let and other obligations entered into by federal agencies in 1951 almost doubled from the level of the previous year.[11]

The fiscal year 1951 witnessed the most rapid and widely pervasive inflationary movement in recent American history with the exception of the decontrol period following the end of World War II. The wholesale price index rose 7 per cent during the first three months of the buildup, an annual rate of 28 per cent.[12]

The following year, fiscal 1952, was the period of the actual major increase in United States military expenditures during the Korean War; it also was a time of comparative stability in the American economy. An examination of the Korean War period discloses several interesting points (see Table 6–2).

TABLE 6–2   *Relationship of Measures of Federal Spending to Activity during the Korean War*
(Per Cent Changes from Previous Period)

Fiscal Year	GNP	Appropriations	Obligations Incurred	Expenditures
1951	+19	+68	+92	+11
1952	+18	+10	+25	+15
1953	+ 4	−12	− 6	+14
1954	+ 1	−24	−23	− 9

SOURCE: *Survey of Current Business*, "1954 National Income Supplement," pp. 222–223, July 1956, pp. 26–27; Murray L. Weidenbaum, "The Economic Impact of the Government Spending Process," *University of Houston Business Review* (Spring 1961).

1. The acceleration in economic activity occurred at approximately the same time as the appropriations were made and the most rapid increase in military orders was taking place.

2. The acceleration in economic activity ceased when the rise in appropriations and obligations (new contract awards) ended.

3. The rise in economic activity virtually ceased when the level of appropriations and obligations began declining.

4. The major rise in government expenditures occurred after the most rapid expansion in economic activity and continued until the decline in appropriations and contract awards.

As it turned out, the direct price, wage, and material controls were imposed after much of the inflationary pressure was over. We may speculate as to whether prompter imposition of tighter monetary and fiscal policies during the fiscal year 1951 would have reduced the inflationary pressures, as well as obviating the need for direct controls.

The Korean experience did show that the strongest inflationary pressures occurred during the first year of the buildup, while the economy was initially adjusting to the new level of military demand which was felt most immediately in the private and not in the public sector of the economy. If there is any economic lesson to be gained from the Korean experience, it is that the nation particularly needs to understand the timing of the impact of the different stages of an increase in government purchases from the private sector. Otherwise, the United States can find itself fighting yesterday's inflation with a tax increase that will compound tomorrow's recessionary problems.

The Vietnam Experience

After a long and happy honeymoon during 1964–1965, the New Economics hit rough seas in 1966, and the marriage between it and the Old Politics began heading toward the rocks in 1967–1968. Post mortems are always difficult. Nevertheless, it is clear in retrospect that a major cause of the difficulties was the economic problems emanating from the Vietnam War.[13]

Economic policy-makers in late 1965 and early 1966 first failed to appreciate the swiftness with which the expansion of the United States commitment in Vietnam was affecting the level of aggregate domestic demand. Then they delayed in initiating stabilizing action promptly enough. Meanwhile, inflationary pressures developed in the American economy which wreaked all sorts of economic and political havoc, ranging from the virtual elimination of the wage-price guidelines to the collapse of effective federal budgetary policy during 1967.

A brief review of the economic problems accompanying the Vietnam buildup evokes memories of the Korean experience. For example, the CEA was able to point with pride to a budget surplus of over $3 billion during the first half of 1966 (at seasonally adjusted annual rates).[14] This naturally was interpreted as indicating the presence of federal fiscal restraint and the absence of any need for tighter monetary or fiscal policy to deal with any war-induced inflation.

The false sense of fiscal security that resulted turned out to be most unfortunate. For, simultaneously, the federal government's demand for the resources of the economy was accelerating to meet the needs of the Vietnam War—and far more rapidly than the rise in tax collections. One indication was that military contract awards in the first 6 months of 1966 were up over a third from the first half of 1965. Also, draft calls rose sharply, to 163,000 for the half year, compared to 62,100 during the first 6 months of 1965. Yet another indicator of the rapid use in government demand was the substantial increase in the amount of raw materials reserved for defense work. For example, aluminum set-asides rose from a quarterly rate of 128,000,000 pounds all through 1965 to 215,000,000 pounds in the first quarter of 1966 and 260,000,000 pounds in the second. The net result was that the federal government, though apparently following a noninflationary economic policy in 1966, was actually a major source of inflationary pressure in the American economy during that time. However, this was only evident to those who took proper account of the extent to which the early and direct impact of the Vietnam buildup was registering in the private sector, rather than the public sector itself.

The Post-Vietnam Economy

In retrospect, it can be argued that a major error occurred in domestic policy in the United States during 1966. The failure of the nation either to understand how massive changes in government purchases from the private sector affect the economy, much less to take prompt and effective compensatory action where necessary, does not augur well for smooth economic adjustments to future changes in government procurement of large magnitude, such as a downturn in military procurement following the termination of hostilities in Vietnam. The deflationary impact of defense contract cancellation and layoffs of defense workers might occur while defense expenditures and/or deliveries were still rising. If tax reduction or monetary ease or expansion in selected nondefense spending programs were to wait until sizable declines in military purchases showed up in the GNP, government economic policy once again would be too slow and too late. Economic analysts and policy-makers need to develop a better understanding of the role of governmental activities in the American economy, particularly of the timing and the location of the economic impacts.

It is always hazardous to forecast future economic events. The past is surely littered with the failures of prognosis. Nevertheless, it appears that—under most scenarios of a post-Vietnam economy —the intertwining of the public and private sectors will continue. That is, some of the savings resulting from a lower level of active military hostilities is likely to be funneled into domestic programs which the federal government operates through contracting out to existing or new private sector mechanisms or delegates to state and local governments, through a variety of financing arrangements. Hence, the issues with which we have been concerned here are likely to become of even greater significance in the years ahead.

NOTES

1. *Survey of Current Business,* July 1967, p. 30.
2. *Survey of Current Business,* "National Income, 1954 Edition," pp. 208–209.
3. Letter to the author from Charles A. Waite, of the National Income Division of the U.S. Department of Commerce, dated June 26, 1968.
4. U.S. Department of Health, Education, and Welfare, *The Research Program of the Social Security Administration* (Washington, D.C.: U.S. Government Printing Office, 1968), pp. 13–14.
5. Agency for International Development, *The Foreign Assistance Program: Annual Report to the Congress, Fiscal Year 1967* (Washington, D.C.: Government Printing Office, 1967), p. 17.
6. Office of Business Economics, Department of Commerce, *The Balance of Payments of the United States, 1949–1951* (Washington, D.C.: U.S. Government Printing Office, 1952), p. 19.
7. *Survey of Current Business,* "National Income, 1954 Edition," pp. 146–147.
8. Office of the Assistant Secretary of Defense (Public Affairs), *Statement Summarizing Actions by the Department of Defense Serving to Reduce the Net Foreign Exchange Costs of Defense Activities During the Period FY 1961–FY 1967,* January 4, 1968, pp. 19–20.
9. U.S. Defense Production Administration, *Defense Production Record,* May 15, 1952, p. 1.; U.S. Congress, Senate, Committees on Armed Services and Appropriations, *Supplemental Military Procurement and Construction Authorizations, Fiscal Year 1967* (Washington, D.C.: U.S. Government Printing Office, 1967), p. 163.
10. Bureau of the Budget, *Budget of the United States Government for the Fiscal Year Ending June 30, 1954* (Washington, D.C.: U.S. Government Printing Office, 1953), p. M6.
11. Murray L. Weidenbaum, "The Economic Impact of the Government Spending Process," *University of Houston Business Review* (Spring 1961), p. 36.
12. *Survey of Current Business,* "1955 Statistical Supplement," pp. 26–27 (base of 1947–1949 = 100).
13. Much of the material in this section is drawn from Murray L. Weidenbaum, "Indicators of Military Demand," *1967 Proceed-*

ings of the Business and Economic Statistics Section (Washington, D.C.: American Statistical Association, 1968).

14. *Cf.* Arthur Okun, "National Defense and Prosperity" (Remarks before the American Ordnance Association, Washington, D.C., October 12, 1966).

7

MICROECONOMIC IMPACTS:
ALLOCATING RESOURCES IN
THE NEW PUBLIC SECTOR

Virtually every appraisal of federal budgeting—that is, of the formal process by which the federal government allocates the resources available to it—concludes that fundamental shortcomings exist. The unanimity on this score embraces government officials and private experts, economists and accountants, liberals and conservatives, and Democrats and Republicans. Disagreements arise, of course, as to the specific improvements to be adopted. There certainly has been no dearth of suggestions for budgetary reform. As we will see, few of them seem to take account of the evolution of the federal establishment from a hirer of clerks and purchaser of paper clips to the source of massive awards of specialized contracts, grants to fifty states and hundreds of localities, and transfer payments and other disbursements to millions of private individuals and organizations.

Organizational Adjustments

Of the many suggestions for improving the allocation of government funds that have been made over the years, the great

155

majority consists of proposals to change the congressional organization for budgetary review. The Legislative Reorganization Act of 1946 made one of the most ambitious efforts along these lines. Section 138 of the Act created a joint committee composed of the two houses of Congress, which was charged with comparing the total receipts and total expenditures proposed in the budget for the coming year, and then recommending a ceiling on expenditures to serve as a control over the total amount of appropriations to be enacted.[1] Section 138 proved unworkable and has been ignored.

New Congressional Committees

Many of the more recent suggestions for changes also are in terms of establishing another congressional committee. A joint committee on the budget or on fiscal policy has often been advocated in order to give overall consideration to revenues, appropriations, expenditures, and debt management by Congress as a whole. Other specific legislative proposals introduced to change the organization or structure of Congress have included a joint congressional committee to audit all government agencies, a Committee on Fiscal Planning for the House of Representatives, and a select committee to study the fiscal and budget organizations and operations of Congress.[2] Either or both houses of Congress has consistently opposed these and similar proposals. The proposed joint committees generally have been turned down in the House of Representatives, which is concerned with maintaining its primacy on financial matters. Attempts to establish new committees in either house have failed because they have been interpreted as diluting the powers of the appropriations committees.

Procedural Adjustments

Another family of suggested improvements in federal government budgeting covers omnibus appropriation bills, special sessions, joint hearings, and similar procedural changes. These proposals require departures from either the way in which Congress meets to consider the budget or in the nature of appropriation legislation.

The House Appropriations Committee did adopt an omnibus appropriation bill for all civilian departments for the fiscal year 1951. However, because of delays and the ease of adding legislative "riders" to such a bill without fear of veto, the following year Congress returned to the old procedure of reporting separate appropriation bills for groups of related departments and agencies.

Other procedural suggestions have included joint hearings by the appropriations committees of both houses, a regular annual budget session of Congress to be held separately from the session on other legislative matters, and a requirement that Congress stay in session until it balances the budget. The last one conjures up visions of permanent national rule by lame duck legislators.

These various attempts to change congressional budgeting procedures have failed to obtain even the level of support gained by some of the proposals to establish new committees.

Using Economic Analysis

There is another approach to the question of allocating government resources. As many economists have pointed out, the essence of budgeting is the choice among alternatives. The following statement by Professor Arthur Smithies of Harvard University states the matter quite clearly: "Budgeting is essentially an economic problem involving as it does the allocation of scarce resources among almost insatiable and competing demands."[3] Economists have long been interested in identifying policies that would promote economic welfare, specifically by improving the efficiency with which a society uses its resources. Governmental budgeting provides one important example of this concern.[4]

As a general proposition, economists contend that changes

in public policy that would increase the amount of economic output available to the nation may be deemed to increase economic welfare. Hence in appraising specific contemplated action —a government project or expenditure program—we are, from this point of view, asking the double question: Do the gains to the beneficiaries outweigh the losses to the rest of the community? Hence, do the benefits exceed the costs to the economy as a whole? The benefits are in the form of increased production of goods and services, and the costs are in terms of the foregone benefits that would have been obtained by using the resources applied to that project in some other activity.

Formal comparisons of benefits and costs have been made for some time by a few federal agencies, especially the Corps of Engineers and the Bureau of Reclamation in evaluating prospective projects. The sensitivity of the results to key assumptions is a major limitation. For example, using a 50-year period in which to "write off" or amortize an investment may yield a ratio of benefits to costs of 1.4, but increasing the write-off period to 100 years (and making no other basic change) raises the benefit-cost ratio to 1.9. Another crucial assumption is choosing an appropriation discount rate to estimate the current value of the future streams of benefits and costs. For example, using a discount rate of 6 per cent, it can be shown that federal financing of a supersonic transport may generate benefits exceeding costs. However, at a 7 per cent rate, the expected costs exceed the likely benefits. It has been contended by many observers that the repeated use of low discount rates (below what the funds could obtain if invested in the private sector) results in many uneconomical projects being funded.[5]

To the extent that benefit-cost analysis thus has been used to sanctify the so-called pork barrel projects, its usefulness is certainly diminished and its confidence undermined. Nevertheless, it has represented a step forward in the application of objective analysis to the question of allocating governmental resources. Benefit-cost analysis has served as a partial screening device to eliminate obviously uneconomical projects; that is those whose prospective gains are less than estimated costs. It also has provided some basis for ranking and comparing projects—a means of choosing among alternatives.

A related development has been the application of cost-effectiveness analysis to military budget decision-making. Much of the development effort was performed at the Rand Corporation under Air Force auspices. For military programs, ordinarily the benefits or results cannot be expressed in dollar terms. However, the end objective—such as the capability to destroy x number of enemy targets under stipulated conditions—can be expressed in quantitative terms. More important than that, the alternative methods of achieving the objective—y bombers versus z missiles or some combination—can be priced out and a least-cost solution arrived at. This approach has been at the heart of the Planning-Programming-Budgeting System (PPBS) introduced in the Pentagon by former Secretary Robert McNamara and economists Charles Hitch, Alan Enthoven, and their associates.

Under the old or pre-McNamara system, each service competed for a larger share of the defense budget and, within the service totals, strategic weapons such as ICBM's competed for funds for small tactical aircraft even though these items were not substitutes but fulfilled basically different functions. Under the new system, realistic alternatives and close substitutes for performing the same or similar mission are compared with each other (for example, ICBM's compete with submarine-launched strategic missiles for strategic program funds), although different services are involved.

It will be recognized that military cost-effectiveness analysis deals with the basic concern of economists: how to attain a higher level of economic performance with the resources at hand and thus increase the welfare of society.

During the past few years, the major civilian agencies of the federal government have been attempting to establish PPBS. These efforts have utilized benefit-cost analysis, cost-effectiveness studies, and other techniques. Numerous shortcomings have been evident in such preliminary efforts. Nevertheless, an important advance in the application of economic analysis to public sector resource allocation has been accomplished.

In August 1965, President Lyndon Johnson announced "a very new and very revolutionary system of planning and programming and budgeting throughout the vast Federal Government—so that through the tools of modern management the full promise of a finer life can be brought to every American at the lowest possible cost."[6]

Mr. Johnson's announcement simply meant, of course, that the civilian agencies were now going to adopt PPBS, as the military had done under Secretary McNamara. The "newness" of his statement was toned down a week later by the then Budget Director Charles L. Schultze. He stated to a congressional committee that he did "not want to leave anybody with the idea that what we are doing is some revolutionary change. It really is an improvement in what we are doing now, a systemization and routinization, if you will. . . ."[7] This may lead observers to conclude that it took one week for the revolutionary to become routine in the Great Society.

In retrospect, it appears that the PPBS effort, while not living up to extravagant claims, is making a contribution to more enlightened resource allocation in the modern public sector.

Through the combined planning and budgeting process, it is hoped that eventually broad national goals will be reduced to specific program operations and the most economical method of carrying them out identified. Several major steps have to be taken in order to accomplish this rather tall order.[8]

First of all, each federal department or agency must identify the specific national goals which are deemed proper and appropriate for the federal government to seek in its area of operation. There certainly does not exist any officially authorized hierarchy of national goals or objectives, despite public and private efforts to develop some. However, some end purposes are fairly clear and perhaps obvious. Examples are the Department of Labor's efforts to increase employment and the activities of the Department of Commerce to expand American exports.

Each department must then examine specific alternative programs that would help to achieve the broad national goals and objectives in its area of responsibility. For example, the goal to increase employment could be achieved by pumping additional purchasing power into the economy through tax reductions, by retraining the unemployed for jobs in the private sector, or by directly increasing the federal payroll.

In theory, the alternatives that appear to be most promising are selected subject to the various constraints under which the federal agency operates. In practice, agencies are often so severely restricted that the choices are few. The typical department finds itself with little discretion in selecting the best combination of programs to assist in achieving broad national goals. It also receives vague or conflicting congressional guidance about the goals to be attained. However, there often is very clear and precise congressional direction as to which specific programs—and in what amounts and particulars—are to be conducted. For example, high minimum wage rates may heighten rather than lower unemployment, but the Department of Labor's discretion has been eliminated by congressional legislation.

The agency's task often is to infer the goals from the specific programs that Congress has authorized and then to develop new or improved means (other programs) to achieve these goals or objectives.

Each government department then estimates the specific costs of alternative programs (in terms of total resources they would require) in order to compare their efficiency in achieving the goals. For example, would government-operated training centers be cheaper or more effective in reducing unemployment than government subsidies for on-the-job training in private industry? Clearly the earlier efforts to use benefit-cost and cost-effectiveness analysis are proving useful at this stage of decision-making.

Finally, each agency then translates the manpower, facilities, and other resource requirements into the common denominator of budget dollars—all projected at least five years ahead—so that the costs of the programs can be analyzed over a meaningful period and decisions made to implement the PPBS results. The first year of each five-year projection can be the basis for the annual budget submissions. The key to the effective use of PPBS is the extent to which the analysis is incorporated into actual budget decisions.

Long-Term Impacts

As a result of the growing use of benefit-cost analysis, cost-effectiveness analysis, and PPBS generally, the decision-making process in the federal government ultimately may sustain substantial change. In the process, of course, PPBS is likely to undergo many modifications, both in name and in basic concepts.

The composition of the federal budget also is likely to be affected. On the basis of the work done to date, benefit-cost and similar analyses show that certain government programs yield a greater economic return (dollar benefit to the nation) than do others. Federal outlays for education, training and retraining, and health—so-called investments in "human" resources—are likely to yield estimated benefits substantially in excess of total costs. The Public Health Service has estimated a benefit-cost ratio of eight for the eradication of syphilis. The OEO has estimated that certain cancer-control programs can yield benefits from four to nine times their cost. An analysis of vocational training programs in Connecticut yielded benefit-cost ratios for individual classes of workers ranging from three to six.[9]

In contrast, some of the more traditional construction-oriented activities, notably irrigation, power, and other multi-purpose water resource projects, are likely to show up far less favorably in this regard. Corps of Engineers and Bureau of Reclamation projects often have ratios as low as 1.2 and 1.1, indicating that the benefits barely exceed the costs.

Hence, some large-scale shifts from "physical" to "human" capital investments are likely to take place in the federal budget as PPBS unfolds its long-term influence.

Limitations of PPBS

If the PPBS succeeds only in a limited way, it will still represent a major advance in the systematic application of economic analysis to the allocation of public resources. Numerous shortcomings are already evident.

A basic limitation is congressional resistance to this executive branch activity. The PPBS analyses are prepared for the use of department heads, the Bureau of the Budget, and the President. Very little of the information thus far has been contained in the formal budget submissions by the agencies to Congress. Hence, congressional committees still continue to scrutinize the details of agency appropriation requests and to ignore the larger questions of goals, objectives, and alternatives.

This resistance on the part of Congress is quite understandable, although not necessarily desirable. Some members have a stake in the present overlapping and duplication of functions. Even though benefit-cost analysis may show that a specific proposed project is uneconomical (that is, the dollar costs exceed the dollar benefits to the nation), the congressmen from that area may still support it simply as an effort to increase federal aid to their constituents. The entire question of the distribution of the benefits, as contrasted with their total size, is neglected in benefit-cost analysis specifically and in PPBS generally. A latter portion of the chapter deals with this question, which is of political as well as economic significance.

It is premature to judge the likelihood of PPBS succeeding in what it is attempting to do. Will the vast system of reports generate into a wheel-spinning operation, or will the results become a significant factor in public policy formulation? From one viewpoint, it is too ambitious, in that it is attempting to apply economic and systems analysis to all of the vast gamut of civilian government operations simultaneously. Perhaps some pilot studies, or a few test cases in civilian agency work, would have provided a sounder basis on which to proceed.

From another viewpoint, however, the PPBS approach is failing to come to grips with the larger choices in allocating federal funds among different agencies and programs. "Would a dollar be more wisely spent for education or for public works?" This fundamental question is not raised anywhere in the budgetary process at the present time—nor is it likely to be answered or even considered under PPBS as it is presently being implemented. The current emphasis is on choosing among more specific alternatives within the education and public works categories and, furthermore, the choices are restricted to being made within each of the many agencies involved in education or public works.

This limitation is also evident in the historical experience in the area where PPBS has been most widely used, national defense. For example, much effort has gone into comparing proposed ICBM systems with long-range bombers as an alternative means of fulfilling a strategic (that is, general war) requirement. Little, if any, formal attention has been devoted to the larger question of determining the optimum allocation of the military budget between strategic forces and limited war (so-called general-purpose) forces. Yet the latter kind of choice may be the critical or fundamental decision in preparing the military budget.

Governmentwide Program Budgeting

A program budget for the entire United States government can be developed from available budget materials. Such a governmentwide program analysis would permit comparing alternative programs of different agencies for fulfilling broad national goals, rather than merely examining the alternatives available to a single federal agency.

A hypothetical program analysis for the entire federal government can be made up by basing it on the fundamental end purposes for which the various government programs are carried on.[10]

In a world of critical international tensions, the initial purpose that comes to mind is the protection of the nation against external aggression—to maintain the national security. A variety of federal programs exists in this category, ranging from equipping and maintaining our own military establishment to bolstering the armed forces of other nations whom we consider potential allies, to various types of nonmilitary competition, and to negotiating arms control agreements. A second basic national purpose, one also going back to the Constitution, is the promotion of the public welfare. Here, we find the federal government operating in the fields of unemployment compensation, social security, veterans' pensions, and many other such activities. A third major purpose of government programs has received an increasing amount of attention in recent years—economic development. This area covers the various programs to develop our natural resources and transportation facilities, as well as the support of education, health, research and development, and other attempts to increase the growth of the American economy. Finally, there is the routine day-to-day operation of the government, such as the functioning of Congress and the federal courts, the collection of revenues, and the payment of interest on the national debt.

Table 7–1 shows how the requested funds in the federal budget for the fiscal year 1967 are allocated among the four major purposes sketched out above. It may come as no surprise that a large portion of the budget—but substantially less than one-half —is devoted to the national security.

TABLE 7–1 *Rudimentary Program Budget for the U.S. Government*
(Fiscal Year 1967, New Obligational Authority)

Broad Purpose	Amount (billions)	Per Cent
National security	$ 68.1	41
Public welfare	61.3	37
Economic development	19.2	12
Government operations	15.7	10
TOTAL	164.3	100

In contrast, the fact that the great bulk of all nonmilitary spending is devoted to the various welfare programs may not be as widely known. A comparatively small portion is devoted to economic development. An examination of the federal budget and congressional appropriation hearings over the years reveals little systematic attempt to appraise the wisdom or desirability of the overall choice implicitly made in the allocation of government resources among these major alternative uses. It may be mere conjecture to conclude that, possibly, the allocation of funds would have been somewhat different if the appropriation requests had been reviewed with an eye on the total picture, instead of examined as individual appropriation items in relative isolation. Added insight to the possible program choices that can be made, using the type of framework suggested here, may be gained from a somewhat deeper analysis of the content of each of these categories.

National Security

As would be expected, the bulk of the national security budget is devoted to the United States military forces. However, one-fifth of the total is comprised of programs that would promote the national security through somewhat more indirect means, such as conducting nonmilitary forms of competition (NASA and United States Information Agency, USIA) or increasing the military capabilities of friendly nations.

The data in Table 7–2 can be used to indicate the types of "strategic" choices that can be made—or are currently being made by default or accident—in allocating funds for national security. First of all, these various defense-related programs are not currently brought together and viewed as a totality anywhere in the budget process (the groupings are arbitrary and illustrative; some for example may contend that NASA's contribution to American economic development is greater than its national security role).

Hopefully, the approach suggested here would lend itself to first raising and then answering questions such as the following:

Would national security be improved by shifting some or all of the $10 billion for foreign aid and nonmilitary competition to the United States military establishment itself?

Conversely, would the national security be strengthened by moving a proportionately small share of the direct military budget, say $500 million, to USIA or the arms control effort and thereby obtaining proportionately large increases in these latter programs?

Are we putting too much into foreign economic aid and not enough into the space program?

Would the nation be better off if we shifted some of the funds now going to passive (civil) defense to the United States Arms Control and Disarmament Agency? Or vice versa?

TABLE 7–2 *National Security Programs*
(Fiscal Year 1967)

Program Category	Amount (billions)	Per Cent
U.S. military forces	$57.8	85
Scientific competition (NASA)	5.0	7
Foreign nonmilitary activities	3.0	4
Foreign military forces	2.0	3
Political and psychological competition (USIA)	.2	**
U.S. passive defense	.1	**
Arms control and disarmament	*	**
TOTAL	68.1	100

* Less than $50 million.   ** Less than ½ of 1 per cent.

The very existence of the type of information presented here may lead not only to attempts to answer such questions as these, but, more fundamentally, to widen the horizons of budget reviewers.

Public Welfare

Over one-third of the 1967 budget is devoted to programs in the general area of the public welfare. Again, these activities are nowhere brought together so that the various spending programs can be compared against each other. The tabulation of public welfare programs contained in Table 7–3 shows a rather large assortment.

TABLE 7–3 *Public Welfare Programs*
(Fiscal Year 1967)

Program Category	Amount (billions)	Per Cent
Life insurance and retirement	$35.1	57
Unemployment insurance	6.9	11
Assistance to farmers and rural areas	6.0	10
Veterans' compensation and pensions	4.3	7
Public assistance	3.8	6
Urban housing and facilities	2.1	4
Anti-poverty programs	1.7	3
Specialized welfare programs	1.4	2
TOTAL	61.3	100

The various quasi-life insurance, unemployment compensation, and retirement programs receive the bulk of the funds for public welfare. However, this is hardly a conscious decision. The level of expenditure for these programs—such as the Old-Age and Survivors' Insurance System—is predetermined by basic, continuing statutes; they are financed by permanent, indefinite appropriations which are not subject to review during the budget process because they do not even appear in the annual appropriation bills. Hence, it is not surprising that these programs have grown to dominate the nondefense budget, exceeding by far the total outlays for the various economic development programs.

Likewise, the expenditures under the various agricultural price support programs (which dominate the category of "assistance to farmers and rural areas") exceed all of the outlays for the programs of urban housing and anti-poverty combined. Again, the farm subsidy program is generally set by the substantive laws on price supports and farm aid, rather than through annual appropriations.

Also, this level of detail permits some cross-comparisons of government programs which are not currently made. For example, the $1.7 billion for formal efforts to reduce poverty in the United States is substantially less than the $3 billion for foreign economic aid. Would some trade-off between the public welfare and national security areas result in a net advantage? This type of analysis is attempting to answer the fundamental question, "Would an extra dollar (a billion, in the case of the government) be more wisely spent for Program A or for Program B?"

Economic Development

In this exploratory categorization of government programs, a number of activities are listed under the heading "economic development." A good share of them, such as the development of needed natural resources or the improvement of necessary transportation facilities, may contribute to the more rapid growth and development of the American economy. Others, such as various subsidies, may be more questionable. Of course, it is inevitable that any classification will contain some borderline cases.

A brief examination of the composition of the economic development category is revealing (see Table 7–4). Transportation facilities account for the largest single share, and when combined with natural resource development and related aids to business, account for almost two-thirds of the total. A governmentwide program budget would focus attention on questions such as, "Would a shift of funds between transportation and education be advisable?" "Between natural resources and research?" Raising these questions need not be taken as expressing value judgments, but rather as indicating a pattern for governmental decision-making.

As indicated earlier, the inclusion of some of these programs

TABLE 7-4 *Economic Development Programs*
(Fiscal Year 1967)

Program Category	Amount (billions)	Per Cent
Transportation facilities	$5.5	29
Education and general research	4.6	24
Natural resources	4.1	21
Health	3.7	19
Aids and subsidies to business	1.3	7
TOTAL	19.2	100

under the economic development category may be questionable. In the case of natural resource programs, the bulk of the funds is devoted to the dams, power, and related multipurpose projects of the Corps of Engineers and the Bureau of Reclamation. Yet many authorities question the merits of individual projects.

Professor Otto Eckstein of Harvard University has reported the following negative findings: "In the case of at least half of all the projects that are being built, it is unlikely that their effect on national income will be positive. . . . The return on many projects is so low that their net effect will be to reduce the rate of growth of the economy."[11]

Government Operations

The final category of government programs represents the general costs of operating the government, the relatively day-to-day functions. More than 80 per cent of the funds in this category cover the payment of interest on the public debt. The bulk of the remaining outlays for government operations is devoted to collecting internal revenue and the housekeeping activities of the Public Buildings Service and the Federal Supply Service.

Implementation

The incorporation in the President's Budget Message and the annual budget document of the approach here suggested might result in growing congressional and public concern and awareness of the problems of choosing among alternative uses of government funds. In the absence of an automatic market mechanism, such an approach might introduce a healthy degree of competition in governmental resource allocation. In a sense, the adoption of a governmentwide program budget would represent a logical expansion of the program budgeting effort at the Pentagon, which worked across rather than down the traditional departmental lines.

An alternative means of implementation would be for a congressional committee staff to rework the existing budget submissions within this framework for review, say, by the entire appropriations committee prior to their detailed examination of individual appropriation requests. This would permit the parent appropriation committees to set general guidelines and ground rules for the detailed budgetary review performed by the specialized subcommittees. It would also permit a vast improvement over the current situation, in which overall government policy often seems to be the accidental by-product of budget decisions on the various departmental requests—rather than the guiding hand behind those decisions.

The underlying theme of such a program approach to government budgeting is the need to array the alternatives so that deliberate choice may be made among them. It has its counterpart in the private sector. Many families might rush out and spend the Christmas bonus for a new car; a more prudent family may carefully (although subjectively) consider the relative benefits of a new car, a long summer vacation, or remodeling the basement. Similarly, a well-managed company would not impulsively decide to devote an increase in earnings to raising dividends, but would consider in detail the alternative uses of the funds—embarking on a new research program, rebuilding an obsolescent manufacturing plant, or developing a new overseas operation.

Institutional Obstacles

The increased efforts that economists and others have been making in recent years to improve the concepts and procedures for allocating public resources make it especially necessary and desirable to focus greater attention on the obstacles to making these improvements operational. Eliminating, or at least reducing, the obstacles to budgetary reform also may be an important way of keeping down the growth of federal expenditures and, hence, of maintaining the primacy of the private sector. Some of the major barriers to improving public resource allocation are the legal and other institutional constraints that limit the discretion of governmental policy-makers.[12]

For example, under present law it is almost futile to perform benefit-cost or similar analyses which may demonstrate that the government obtains a lower return on its investments in highway transportation than in air transportation or some other alternative and, hence, that some shifting of funds might improve economic welfare. The futility arises from the fact that the major financial authorizations for highway programs are not contained in the appropriation bills requested by the President and enacted by Congress, but in the relatively long-term legislation which authorizes the federal-aid highway program. Thus, Congress cannot, through the budget review and appropriations process, in practice effect a transfer of funds from surface to air transportation by reducing the appropriations for the Bureau of Public Roads and increasing those for the Federal Aviation Agency, two component units of the Department of Transportation.

Similarly, there is no discretion through the budget process to shift funds from an income-maintenance program such as public assistance to aid to education, both functions of HEW—or to any other purpose whether it involves expenditures or tax reduction. This rigidity arises because the expenditures under the public assistance program are in the nature of fixed charges; they are predetermined by statutory formulas governing federal matching of state disbursements for public assistance. Given the permanent statute on the books, the amount that the federal government spends on this income-maintenance activity each year is determined by the pattern of state welfare disbursements. Neither the President nor Congress can much influence the amount of federal expenditures in this area within the confines of the budget process. Changes in the basic social security legislation would be necessary.

There are many, many other examples of these institutional obstacles to improving the allocation of public resources. The end result of course is that the process of public resource allocation is hardly that deliberate and systematic choice among alternatives that economists try to envision. Rather, it is a fragmented and compartmentalized affair. Many of the key decisions are not made during the budget process or within the budgetary framework at all.

It is an earlier stage of the process which is the effective point of decision-making on numerous government spending programs —the enactment of substantive and often permanent legislation. This is the birth stage, and rebirth and growth stages, of a substantial proportion of federal spending. This is the stage where many of the basic policy decisions are made—the nature of farm subsidies, the types of public assistance payments, and the level of highway grants. However, since it is the substantive committees of Congress (for example, commerce, foreign relations, or public works) which handle enabling or authorizing legislation, rather than the appropriations committees, cost implications of the new programs often are relegated to secondary consideration or even ignored. The effectiveness of appropriations control over federal government expenditures is far less than it superficially appears to be.

In practice the President and Congress do not face each year's budget preparation and review cycle with a clean slate; they must take account of large accumulations of legal restraints within which they must operate. There are thus numerous exogenous forces and factors which they must consider and cannot effectively control: the number of eligible veterans who apply for pensions or compensation, the amount of public assistance payments made by the states and for which they must be partially reimbursed according to prescribed matching formulas, and so forth.

Four categories of exogenous institutional barriers to improving (or at least changing) the allocation of government resources can be identified: trust funds, permanent and indefinite appropriations, fixed charges, and ongoing projects. Trust funds vary from the large social insurance type of mechanisms, such as the old-age, survivors', and disability insurance program, to the gift fund for the Library of Congress. The common characteristic of these trust funds is that they are generally financed through permanent appropriations which do not require annual action by Congress. Another clear indication of the relative uncontrollability of these trust funds through the budget process is that they generally do not even appear in the annual appropriation bills. In the case of the social insurance funds, the actual level of expenditures is determined by the number of eligible persons who apply for benefits during a given year.

In addition to the trust funds, there are numerous permanent appropriations which are contained in the budget. The largest of these is the permanent and indefinite appropriation for the payment of interest on the national debt which provides that "such amounts are appropriated as may be necessary to pay the interest each year on the public debt."

Other permanent accounts cover such items as the appropriations to the Department of Agriculture for removal of surplus farm commodities and to the Department of the Interior for range improvements. Of the gross customs receipts, 30 per cent is automatically available to finance the agriculture program each year regardless of estimated need or relative desirability vis-à-vis the changing mix of public sector activities. One-third of grazing revenues from federal lands are similarly available for range improvement work.

A related category of funding is the "indefinite" appropriations. Although these are contained in the annual appropriation bills, they are in the nature of a blank check good for one year. Indefinite appropriations authorize a government agency to spend the sums necessary to meet a given specified requirement. The Post Office Department is financed through such an annual indefinite appropriation.

A third type of a relatively uncontrollable item is often termed a "fixed charge." These are programs where the level of spending is determined effectively by basic statutes rather than through the review of annual appropriation requests. The largest programs of this type are the appropriations for public assistance and for veterans' compensation and pensions. HEW disburses grants to states to reimburse them for a fixed share of the public assistance payments that they make. Similarly, the Veterans Administration provides statutorily determined benefits to all qualifying veterans or their widows and children who apply.

Although programs such as these are funded through annual, definite appropriations, there is little effective control over the actual level of disbursements. Frequently, the initial appropriations turn out to be too low and supplemental appropriations are subsequently requested and routinely approved. There is considerable incentive for Congress to appropriate less than the initial amount requested in the budget for these items. Thus, it gains some political benefit for supposedly "cutting" the budget. They then can later and much more quietly vote supplemental funds.

Another type of relatively uncontrollable budget activity is the amount of new funds requested to continue or complete construction and similar long-term projects started with money voted in the budgets of earlier years. The almost unassailable justification for these appropriations is the old question, "What is the value of just half a bridge?" Typically for government agencies with large construction programs, such as the Army Corps of Engineers and the Department of the Interior, each year's budget request is dominated by funds needed for projects begun under prior year budgets.

In the aggregate, the trust funds, the ongoing construction

projects, and the other permanent and indefinite appropriations and fixed charges account for a major share of the budget—$97.5 billion or 48 per cent of the total budget authority requested in the fiscal year 1969.

Were the fixed charges and other relatively uncontrollable items distributed proportionally to the size of the budgets of the various government agencies, the interference with the allocation of government resources would be at a minimum. However, this is hardly the case. Some agency programs virtually escape the scrutiny of effective annual budgetary review—the Post Office, the Export-Import Bank, the Railroad Retirement Board, the Farm Credit Administration, and the great bulk of the Treasury Department.

At the other end of the controllability spectrum, all or almost the entire annual budgets of the departments of Defense (excluding civil functions such as the Corps of Engineers' construction work), Justice, and State, and the General Services Administration are subject to effective control through the annual budget process.

An interesting contrast appears between the two departments with the largest budgets, one military and the other civilian. The Department of Defense operates with very few and very small trust funds and other fixed charges. Almost all of its budget is subject to annual scrutiny. In comparison, only one-tenth of the HEW budget can effectively be altered during the annual budget cycle. Most of the funds spent are insulated by permanent and indefinite appropriations and other long-term statutory commitments.

The following changes in congressional legislation or procedures would reduce these institutional obstacles to improving the allocation of public resources:

1. *Reduce the number of trust funds.* In many cases—such as the federal-aid highway program—it is hard to make a case for segregating the activity from ordinary budget operations. That particular program of federal grants to the states did operate

out of general revenues until 1954. The highway-related excises which are now funneled through the highway trust fund may be viewed more properly as a form of earmarked taxes and treated within the regular budget procedure.

2. *Review the need for the permanent and indefinite appropriations.* Some of them have outlived their usefulness. However, there is no automatic or periodic review of their status.

3. *Eliminate some of the fixed charges.* Restore discretion to the appropriations committee to determine annually the amount to be voted for the stipulated purpose, in the light of the then current conditions and competing requirements.

4. *Focus greater attention on "new starts" of construction and other long-term projects.* It is a natural tendency to place greater emphasis in the budgetary review process on the items with the largest price tags. However, most of the appropriation requests for long-term projects are to continue or complete projects already underway. The point of most effective control is at the outset, prior to the investment of public resources in the project. However, it is precisely at the starting stage where the appropriation requests are most modest and thus perhaps more readily approved. A careful weighing of the expected full- or long-term costs and benefits is thus extremely important prior to undertaking the project.

The reduction of these institutional obstacles to maximizing the taxpayers' return on their investment will not of itself result in eliminating relatively low priority and less efficient government activity. It should make efforts in that direction less difficult and, in a positive way, permit the federal government to reorient its activities in line with changing needs and requirements.

The Distribution of Benefits

There is an important aspect to public sector resource allocation which is often overlooked by those who focus on simply identifying those alternatives which are likely to produce the greatest excess of dollar benefits over dollar costs—the distribution of the benefits. As was pointed out in Chapter 1, it is possible to develop governmental investment projects which meet the efficiency criterion (that is, the total benefits exceed the total costs), but which fail to meet the simplest standards of equity. In the case of the navigation project cited there, the costs would be widely distributed among taxpayers generally but the benefits would accrue to a single organization at one location. Unfortunately, there has been a tendency on the part of some economists to dismiss such "distributional" questions as subjective and political, and hence not within the proper concern of economic analysis.

If the annual budget of the federal government—about $200 billion—were equally distributed among its citizens, each would find his yearly income increased by about $1,000 in cash and services. Similarly, if the budget were divided equally among the fifty states, each would receive $400 million worth of grants, payments, subsidies, dams, post office clerks, and other forms of federal largesse.

Federal budgets, of course, are not allocated equally, either to people or to states. In fact, these billions of dollars have an important effect on the unequal way in which income is distributed in the United States. Certain government programs allocate funds in such a manner as to increase the existing inequalities of income distribution, while other programs tend to decrease these inequalities.

Which federal programs do what? Does spending by the Department of Defense, for example, contribute to a more equal spread of personal income throughout the country—or does it concentrate money in certain specific places? How does the pattern of defense spending compare with, say, aid to education or grants to states for highway design and construction?

These questions can be answered by taking typical programs within each major category of federal expenditures and comparing their patterns of regional distribution among each other and with those of population and personal income in the United

States.[13] Some of the variations are striking. For example, the relatively high income areas—the Far West, the Mideast, and New England—receive shares of defense contracts which are substantially above both their shares of population and of income. Hence, the regional distribution of defense production reinforces the position of the wealthier regions. In contrast, all of the other regions—the Great Lakes, the Plains, the Rocky Mountains, the Southwest, and the Southeast—receive shares of defense work which are below their shares of population or income.

The regional distribution of NASA procurement also appears to be relatively unequal. All regions, except the Far West and Plains states, receive less than a proportional share (the Southeast receives less than a per capita share but one larger than its proportion of personal income). Undoubtedly, this situation results in large part from the fact that the high-technology aerospace and electronics industries, which produce the bulk of the goods and services that NASA requires, are concentrated in certain areas of the country. Unlike the regional pattern of defense work, there can be little question of a "chicken versus egg" explanation of causation in this case. The locations of the major industrial design and production facilities were established prior to the formation of NASA.

In fact, there is a striking resemblance of the current geographic distribution of civilian space work to the state-by-state distribution of missile employment in 1958, before the beginning of the NASA program. As the civilian space program originated as a technical outgrowth of ICBM and related missile programs, this correspondence should come as no surprise. Actually, the lowest income regions obtain a larger share of NASA contracts than they do of military missile employment.

Quite different patterns emerge when we examine civilian government programs, requiring lower levels of science and technology. For example, although the operations of the Corps of Engineers cover all fifty states, major new projects for navigation, flood control, hydroelectric power, and similar purposes are centered in the western and southern regions—the Far West, the Southeast, the Plains, and the Southwest, in that order. Various reasons may be offered for this geographical pattern. Corps-of-Engineer operations in the older areas, such as the Mideast, New England, and Great Lakes, are in a more advanced state, requiring mainly operation and maintenance and relatively little new construction. Also, costs of potential new projects may be extremely high in these greatly populated areas and benefit-cost analyses of proposed new projects may not show favorable results.

Similarly, the four regions with the lowest average per capita incomes—the Southeast, the Southwest, the Rocky Mountains, and the Plains—receive larger shares of federal highway funds than would correspond either to their shares of income or population. This apparently reflects the tendency for areas with low average incomes to have a low population density and, hence, to benefit more than proportionately from program expenditures determined on a spatial basis. Three of the higher income regions received lower than average per capita shares; these were all in the East—the Mideast, New England, and the Great Lakes. The share of highway funds received by the Far West was slightly higher than what would have been the result of a straight per capita distribution, but slightly lower than its corresponding share of total income.

A major feature of the relatively new legislation for aid to elementary and secondary education is the financial assistance to school districts with a high proportion of low-income families. It is apparent that the legislation does achieve an anti-poverty objective by channeling funds in a major way to low-income areas. With the exception of the Rocky Mountain states the lower income regions receive substantially larger shares of the education grants than would be indicated by their population or income ratios. The four higher income regions, conversely, receive significantly lower shares than would result from a distribution based either on population or income. This emphasis on low-income states exceeds all other programs here examined, except agricultural subsidies.

As would be expected, the bulk of the farm subsidies (the agricultural price support payments made by the United States Department of Agriculture) goes to the regions with large agricultural sectors, particularly those devoted to the major supported crops—corn, wheat, sorghum grain, tobacco, cotton, and peanuts. Also, the agricultural states are generally in the lower income areas. Hence, there is a striking correspondence between farm-price support payments, and low-income areas. Over half of the funds are channeled to the southwestern and southeastern states which, by way of comparison, receive less than one-fourth of total personal income and have slightly less than 30 per cent of the national population.

Veterans' benefit payments (compensation to veterans with service-connected disabilities and pensions to other needy veterans) are fairly equally distributed throughout the country. Each of the four lower income regions receives a slightly more than proportionate share of the federal funds. Conversely, three out of the four higher income regions (the exception being New England) receive slightly less than a proportionate share of such payments.

The four lower income regions received a substantially larger proportion of public assistance payments than their share of either population or income. However, only two out of the four higher income regions—the Mideast and the Great Lakes— had lower shares of public assistance payments than of either income or population.

All of the programs analyzed are progressive, that is, reduce the inequality in the distribution of personal income among regions, except for the two making the greatest use of high technology and, thus, highly skilled factors of production—the defense and space programs.

Thus, the spatial pattern of distribution of most federal non-defense programs tends to reduce regional income inequality

The policy implications are quite clear—the continued expansion in conventional, domestic, civilian programs will tend to reduce the disparities in income among the different areas of the country. Some of these programs may be more effective in this regard than others (education versus public works), but they all seem to tend in the same direction of greater equality of income distribution.

In general, the low-income states tend to receive a larger than proportional share of expenditures for the nondefense programs. This reflects, of course, the welfare orientation implicit or explicit in so many of these programs. In contrast, the high-income states tend to receive a larger than proportional share of expenditures for defense and space programs, thus reflecting the dependence on the highly industrialized areas for the design and production of weapon and space systems.

Hence, a shift in the federal budget from defense to non-defense activities—assuming no fundamental alteration in the geographic distribution patterns of individual public programs —tends to narrow income inequality among the various regions of the United States. Conversely, a shift to defense programs tends to widen the range of income inequality among regions.

The policy implication would seem to be quite clear. The continued expansion of military and related procurements from high-technology, government-oriented corporations is increasing the disparities in income among the different areas of the country. Following peace in Vietnam, the nation would have the opportunity to redress the balance, but only if it consciously allocates funds to programs that benefit the poorer regions at least proportionally, if not even to a greater degree.

The different geographic impacts of the various instruments available to carry out national policies are also striking and need to be taken account of in post-Vietnam economic planning. The choice among contracts with government-oriented corporations, grants to the states, transfer payments, and direct federal operations imply powerfully different regional distributions of federal money.

The large corporations with the major concentrations of scientific and engineering capabilities tend to cluster in the highly industrialized areas of the Middle Atlantic and Pacific Coastal states. Federal contracts to these organizations tend to bolster the incomes of these already above-average areas in terms of economic wealth.

Moreover, the limited data that are available tend to indicate that these government-oriented corporations generate relatively larger numbers of jobs for the most highly skilled and, hence, most highly paid employees and proportionately fewer semi-skilled jobs for persons with less training and education.

In 1967, the United States Labor Department reported only 10 per cent of defense jobs were in the low-paid laborer or service categories, compared to over 22 per cent for manufacturing as a whole. At the other end of the income spectrum, 61 per cent of defense jobs were in the professional and skilled worker classifications, and only 45 per cent for total manufacturing.[14]

In contrast, grants-in-aid to state and local governments tend to be distributed more in proportion to the population at large and to be channeled, either directly or indirectly, to persons with lower incomes (the unemployed, road construction workers, public school teachers, librarians, and so forth). The states with lowest per capita incomes—those in the southern and southwestern regions—receive disproportionately large shares of the federal grant funds. However, as was shown in Chapter 4, different federal-aid formulas would alter considerably the geographic allocation of these funds. As we have seen, direct federal transfer payments and federal employment tend to be fairly proportionately distributed with reference to population.

Summary

It would appear that many further improvements are needed in the methods whereby public sector resources are allocated among the different programs. Examining each bureau and program in isolation—either at the Budget Bureau or congressional level—is an inadequate way of dealing with the modern, intertwined public sector. Moreover, in an economy where the federal government is a major transferer of income from one group of the population to another, it is no longer feasible to ignore these "subjective" or "distributional" questions in putting together or enacting the federal budget. Rather, modern governmental budgeting should begin with a firm understanding of the changing nature of the public sector and then develop the tools of budgeting commensurate with these needs.

Program budgeting represents a major step in that direction. However, it needs to be applied across the board, covering the entire gamut of governmental activities, so that comparisons can be made among programs conducted by federal agencies, those contracted out to government-oriented corporations or private nonprofit institutions, those in a sense delegated to state or local governments, and those involving direct federal payments to the ultimate beneficiaries. Hence, at the broadest level, the allocation of federal resources must take account simultaneously of the distribution by program, by region, and by income class as well as by performing mechanism. This is hardly a task to be relegated to some clerks with high-speed computers at their disposal. Rather, it calls for judgment and understanding at the highest levels.

Perhaps a bit bombastic, William Gladstone, the nineteenth-century British prime minister, nevertheless captured the essence in his classic statement, "Budgets are not mere affairs of arithmetic, but in a thousand ways go to the root of prosperity of individuals, and relation of classes, and the strength of kingdoms."

NOTES

1. U.S. Congress, Senate, Committee on Government Operations, *Create a Joint Committee on the Budget,* Hearings on S. 537 (Washington, D.C.: U.S. Government Printing Office, 1963).
2. U.S. Congress, Senate, Committee on Government Operations,

Financial Management in the Federal Government (Washington, D.C.: U.S. Government Printing Office, 1962).

3. Arthur Smithies, *The Budgetary Process in the United States* (New York: McGraw-Hill, Inc., 1955), pp. xiv–xv.

4. Some of the following material is based on Murray L. Weidenbaum, "Economic Analysis and Government Expenditure Decisions," *Finanzarchiv* (November 1966).

5. U.S. Congress, Joint Economic Committee, *Economic Analysis of Public Investment Decisions: Interest Rate Policy and Discounting Analysis* (Washington, D.C.: U.S. Government Printing Office, 1968), p. 20.

6. The White House, *Introduction of New Government-Wide Planning and Budgeting System*, August 25, 1965, p. 3.

7. U.S. Congress, Joint Committee on the Organization of Congress, "Statement of Charles L. Schultze," *Organization of Congress*, Part 12 (Washington, D.C.: U.S. Government Printing Office, 1965), p. 1799.

8. This section is drawn from statements by then Budget Director Charles L. Schultze in *ibid.*, pp. 1775–1835, and U.S. Congress, Joint Economic Committee, *Fiscal Policy Issues of the Coming Decade* (Washington, D.C.: U.S. Government Printing Office, 1965), pp. 59–96.

9. Michael E. Borus, "A Benefit-Cost Analysis of the Economic Effectiveness of Retraining the Unemployed," *Yale Economic Essays* (Fall 1964).

10. An earlier version of this analysis appears in Murray L. Weidenbaum, "Which Resources for What Goals: Another Look at the Budget," *Challenge* (June 1964).

11. Otto Eckstein, "Evaluation of Federal Expenditures for Water Resource Projects," U.S. Congress, Joint Economic Committee, *Federal Expenditure Policy for Economic Growth and Stability* (Washington, D.C.: U.S. Government Printing Office, 1957), p. 667.

12. See Murray L. Weidenbaum, "On the Effectiveness of Congressional Control of the Public Purse," *National Tax Journal* (December 1965), pp. 370–374.

13. The data are taken from Murray L. Weidenbaum, "Shifting the Composition of Government Spending: Implications for the Regional Distribution of Income," *Regional Science Association Papers*, Vol. XVI (1966).

14. Max A. Rutzick, "Worker Skills in Current Defense Employment," *Monthly Labor Review* (September 1967), pp. 17–18.

8

THE FUTURE STRUCTURE OF THE PUBLIC SECTOR

As we have seen, the federal government's activities related to the national security have been conducted in quite a distinct manner from the domestic welfare programs. The one relies heavily on advanced science and technology made available through industrial corporations. The other uses mainly conventional methods (brick and mortar and transfer payments) and operates in large measure through state and local governments. Entrenched patterns of operation would indicate continuance of the status quo.

Increasingly, however, the newer and emerging areas of government activity are creating demands for merging the two mechanisms, for involving both industry and local government in such problems as poverty, environment pollution, urban transportation, and so forth. The limits to which the federal government can effectively conduct programs affecting all fifty states and hundreds of metropolitan areas are becoming readily apparent in a variety of domestic areas.

An obvious case is the postal service. In part, because of its relatively low level of mechanization and its limited use of new technology, the Post Office is showing increasing difficulty in carrying on its function of delivering the mail. A Presidential commission recently has recommended that the functions of the Post Office Department be turned over to a public corporation patterned after the Tennessee Valley Authority. A move to a corporate form would give the Post Office greater discretion to set rates and to invest in the application of new technology and capital facilities to its presently very labor-intensive operations.

Much more attention has been given to the possibilities of setting up one or more quasi-governmental or government-sponsored corporations in an effort to utilize private industry in rebuilding urban ghetto areas. The interest in some type of federally related corporation arises, of course, from the desire to assign a portion of the risk of financing requirements to the federal Treasury.

The National Corporation for Housing Partnerships was created during the last days of the Johnson administration to foster construction of low-cost housing. However, it appears that no partnerships will be set up until the federal government insures an adequate supply of tenants via rent subsidies. As of early 1969, the National Corporation had succeeded in attracting heads of major corporations to its Board of Directors (Westinghouse Electric Corporation, Metropolitan Life Insurance Company, Penn-Central Railroad, Kaiser Industries, Lazard Frères and Company, and others of that stature). However, the total amount of private capital that was raised came to $1.5 million and required a consortium of fifteen of the nation's largest banks to do so.[1]

It would thus appear that these companies are more eager to serve as agents of the federal government than to embark upon truly private risk-bearing activities. It is easy of course to be unduly harsh. The intent of the federal program is to induce private enterprise to take on the construction of homes for a market which does not appear to be attractive or even profitable in the absence of federal assistance.

The Spectrum of Alternatives
Available to the Federal Government

There is a spectrum of alternative mechanisms which the federal government can utilize in carrying out its functions. These vary from direct employment of civil servants to the more indirect forms involving private sector organizations or individuals, subject to varying degrees of federal direction, control, or influence.

From the viewpoint of the federal official, direct employment of civil servants in carrying out national programs has advantages not possessed by the other alternatives. These employees are subject to their direct supervision and control and have no other allegiance. When relying on their own work forces, federal officials do not need to be so concerned with the desires of governors, mayors, and other elected officers, as in the case of grants-in-aid, or in the operating manner of private managers, as in the case of contracts with the private sector. By using their own employees federal officials are freer to rely on their own judgments as to what are the national interests to be served in various programs.

However, the very size of federal operations and their multiplicity make difficult any effective execution of national objectives in a given region. The question of pollution of Lake Michigan furnishes a current and perhaps classic example of the inability of the federal bureaucracy to deal with local or even regional problems. It turns out that the rivers and harbors work of the Army Corps of Engineers requires it to dredge ports from time to time in order to keep them in proper condition. The wastes dredged up present a large disposal problem. In the case of projects in the vicinity of Lake Michigan, apparently the Corps has "solved" the problem by dumping the wastes in Lake Michigan, thereby aggravating a growing pollution problem in that great body of water. In response to appeals by the federal agencies responsible for health and water pollution (HEW and the Interior), the Corps has steadfastly denied that it is causing pollution. It does admit that it is moving pollutants from adjoining rivers into the lake, but it contends that it is not doing the pollution, but merely transferring it from one site to another!

Attempts of congressmen and senators from the area—from both major political parties—to deal with the sophistry of this argument have proved unsuccessful. The Corps passes the buck back to the Bureau of the Budget. The bureau has given luke-warm or negative endorsements to many of the Corps of Engineers' projects in the first place (through the legislative clearance process). A feeling of nearly complete hopelessness fills almost anyone reading the pertinent testimony of federal officials before the congressional committees.[2]

Via the award of contracts the federal government can bring into its employ business firms, nonprofit organizations, and even individuals, all lodged in the private sector of the economy. Contracts enable the federal government to specify fairly precisely the nature of the activity to be performed in the private sector, as well as the method of its performance.

Via the disbursement of grants-in-aid, federal agencies can also obtain the involvement of state and local governments and nonprofit organizations, as well as individuals. However, the ease of supervision and control is less than under the contract device, although that is mainly a matter of degree. Specific conditions can and are established before a recipient can receive various types of federal grants.

Generally, the most "private" end of the spectrum is expenditures for benefit payments, such as veterans' compensation and pensions, Old-Age and Survivors' Insurance, and unemployment compensation. In all of these cases, the recipient is free to spend the federal money as he wishes. He is subject neither to advance approval of his expenditure plans nor of post-audit of his use of the federal money. (As we have seen, however, Medicare is an exception to this: the federal government makes payments in behalf of an individual for a specified listing of expenses.)

In some sense, many of these private sector or other nonfederal organizations may lose some of their "privateness" in dealing with the federal government. To what extent can we call "private" an organization that regularly receives over 90 per cent of its business from a small number of federal agencies; whose long-term and working capital is largely supplied by these agencies; whose prices are determined not in the open market but in negotiations with governmental buyers, who are required unilaterally to set specific standards for contract negotiation and execution; and whose profits (in the case of the corporations) are subject to after-the-fact reduction by the Federal Renegotiation Board on the basis of quite general standards? Is nominal private ownership a facade for public control and direction? Are the government-oriented corporations effectively agents of the federal government?

On the basis of the evidence to date, the answers to these questions must be inconclusive. The close, day-to-day surveillance by government agencies has been reducing the entrepreneurial character of the private corporations with which the government deals, but it has not eliminated the vital private characteristics. Moreover, some "counterattacks" are evident from time to time. A few government-oriented corporations have been merging with firms entrenched in commercial markets in an effort to reduce their dependence on government markets. Others have been attempting to develop overseas markets. Many federal contractors have simultaneously been seeking business with state and local governments and in some selected industrial or consumer product areas.

Hence, it does not seem that it can truthfully be said that these government-oriented corporations and other organizations have generally become complete agents of the federal government, and thus lost all of their private character. Yet, they are subject to more direct and close public control and direction than are other segments of the private economy. It certainly is not an either-or type of situation, but the side effects of the close government-industry relationship need to be recognized and to be borne in mind in developing public policy, particularly in extending the use of the private corporation in civil public sector programs.

Federal credit programs furnish a warning or at least an example of how nominal private ownership can become a facade for governmental control. For example, a number of agricultural banking-type operations—the Federal Land Banks, the Federal Intermediate Credit Banks, and the Federal Home Loan Banks— were originally set up as federal corporations. The private users of these facilities were required to purchase capital stock in them as part of the "price" charged. As gradually the federal capital was retired and replaced by private capital, the banks became more in the nature of private institutions. However, the status of these government-sponsored corporations has remained a cloudy one. Their bonds are often tax-exempt, they continue to have a line of credit with the federal Treasury, and the federal government maintains some financial or administrative controls over them.[3] Their "gray" status can be seen from the fact that some measures of federal government expenditures have included all of these government-sponsored corporations (the consolidated cash statement), some have not included any (the administrative or conventional budget), and some have included a few but excluded others (the new unified budget and the "national income accounts" budget).

The secondary mortgage operation of the Department of Housing and Urban Development (conducted via the Federal National Mortgage Association, FNMA) represents an interesting and current case of changing status. Originally, a "wholly owned" federal enterprise, FNMA (or Fannie Mae, as it is often called) has become a "mixed-ownership" corporation during recent years as the users of its services have been required to provide a portion of the equity capital. Those selling mortgages to Fannie Mae are required to buy an amount of stock equal to 1 per cent of the unpaid principal amount of the mortgages sold. An effort is now under way to retire the remaining government capital. Despite the transition in ownership, the federal government would retain considerable influence on FNMA through its ability to borrow over $2 billion from the Treasury and through a board of directors composed partially of government appointees.[4]

Dr. Arnold Diamond, a close student of these government-sponsored corporations, points out that, because they are vested with "vital functions of national concern, their private owners have virtually no voice in the policy decisions of these institutions." After careful analysis of the major agencies which have made the transition from public ownership to nominal private ownership, Dr. Diamond concludes that their internal decision-making is the province of "public officials accountable to the President or to the Congress."[5]

Grants-in-aid, particularly to state and local governments, present an even less clear-cut case. Certainly, the states maintain that they are still very much sovereign in our federal form of government. Yet, federal grants do influence, in some cases very strongly, the program areas where attention and resources are to be devoted. Some of the newer proposals, such as block grants or tax sharing, are far more than methods of channeling federal funds to the states; they would reduce the extent to which federal agencies control or at least strongly influence state and local programs and policies.

Private nonprofit organizations doing most of their work for federal departments and agencies, whether financed by outright contracts or via grants-in-aid, tend to present problems similar to those of the government-oriented corporations. Private individuals who depend on federal grants or contracts for large shares of their income may in some cases adopt the attitudes of career civil servants who refrain from publicly criticizing federal policies and programs.

If any conclusion can be arrived at with considerable confidence, it is that in selecting among the array of alternative mechanisms available, federal policy-makers should not be totally oblivious of their effects on the basic structure of these mechanisms. In areas such as engineering, education, health, social work, and transportation—where the federal government is a major source of financing—ignoring the longer term side effects may significantly and adversely affect the basic capabilities of these organizations. One obvious solution is to reduce federal dependence on any single mechanism, whether it is corporations or other levels of government or nonprofit institutions. Perhaps an even more fundamental answer is to shift the solution of the basic problems to these other segments of society.

Tax sharing, federal tax incentives to private industry, general lowering of the levels of governmental taxation, and untied transfer payments all represent ways of channeling more resources to these other segments of society. Certainly, with the greater autonomy over these funds by the recipients, there will be a corresponding reduction in federal influence and control. Perhaps, there also will be some reduction in the extent to which these resources are used to meet the problems which national decision-makers consider to merit highest priority. But that, of course, is the basic trade-off or choice between national control, on the one hand, and local and private initiative, on the other.

Other differences that arise from the use of these alternative devices also need to be recognized. In the very real sense that they all represent ways of using the financial resources available to the national government, tax reductions, grants to states, transfer payments, and contracts with government-oriented corporations are alternative devices for achieving national objectives.

Further reliance on the corporate form would probably utilize science and technology to the most substantial degree. It also would involve federal agencies and private organizations in close and continuing if not intertwined relationships. It would create opportunities for innovation in establishing programs and creativity in the method of their execution. It is likely that substantial investments in capital (both physical and human) would be made. Also, this approach might well result in the average citizen affected dealing with a variety of large organizations that he neither understands too well nor knows how to influence or control effectively, at least at the outset.

In contrast, negative income taxes or other transfer payments ("government handouts," to use the vernacular) would mainly increase consumer purchasing power. Probably the funds would be utilized in more conventional ways—for family purchases of food, clothing, household appliances, entertainment, and so forth. A greater role would be played by the private market. Research and development and other capital investments would occur to a lesser degree and only indirectly as the suppliers to the consumers' market saw opportunity for making such expenditures. A relative decline in the size of the public sector of the economy would occur as a greater share of output would be produced in the private sector and sold directly to individual customers. Perhaps, the role of the tax investigator would become a more important one.

The choice between public and private emphasis in achieving basic national purposes is not likely to be an easy or quick one. The advantages and disadvantages of each route are substantial. The Bureau of the Budget, in exercising its role as the President's managerial arm, has been attempting to define the limits of federal in-house activity as well as of contracting out. Of necessity, its directives thus far have been couched in quite general language.

In a directive first issued during the Eisenhower administration, the bureau instructed the federal agencies not to start up or continue "commercial-industrial" activities if the product or service involved could be procured from private enterprise. Inevitably, exceptions were authorized, particularly if required for national security purposes or if the government could supply the item itself more cheaply.[6]

The major effect of the bureau bulletin was to terminate military rope and paint installations and similar relatively small and minor activities. Perhaps the most important impact of the bulletin was more difficult to measure, the establishment of the presumption that the public sector would generally rely on the private sector for the production of goods and services required to operate the government.

At the other end of the spectrum, and more recently, the

Bureau of the Budget has indicated the circumstances under which so-called management and operating contracts could be entered into by federal agencies. These arrangements cover such contracted-out activities as running national laboratories (for the AEC), monitoring the development of new weapon systems (for the Air Force), and operating testing facilities (for NASA).

Again in vaguely defined terms, the bureau came closest to stating basic philosophy governing the types of federal functions which could not be performed by the private sector:

1. Directing, supervising, and controlling government personnel, except when incidental to training.

2. Exercising police and regulatory powers in the name of the government, except guard and protection services.

3. Determining basic government policies.

4. Day-to-day staff and management functions, such as internal personnel administration and budget preparation.[7]

In practice, fine lines are difficult to draw. Nonprofit research organizations may not formally determine basic government policies, but the sponsoring agency may find it difficult to turn down their recommendations on highly technical questions. The management consultants may not prepare the actual budget submissions for a government agency, but their forecasts and program analyses may be the fundamental bases for the budget estimates. Government-oriented corporations may not be exercising police powers, but their operating of Job Corps camps may be a fairly close approximation.

The General Accounting Office, in its continual audits of government operations, has attempted to define the limits of what it terms "work traditionally performed by government employees." One of the few relatively clear-cut decisions of the General Accounting Office in this area was rendered in 1952 when the Navy was barred from using contracts to assist in administering procurement contracts, including the application of financial controls and audits. It apparently was too great a stretch of the imagination to contract out major aspects of the very process by which the government contracts out some of its activities.

Nevertheless, in a detailed study of this phenomenon, Clarence Danhof has concluded that the General Accounting Office's "defense" of the boundaries of "work traditionally performed by government employees" has been "highly permissive."[8]

The Dominant Trends

Several dominant trends are likely to persist in the public sector of the United States during coming decades. In view of continuing racial tensions, the emphasis on urban problems will probably increase and outlays for people-oriented programs (so-called investments in human capital) will grow. Wider uses will be found for the results of science and new technology in domestic programs. Virtual stability in federal employment will continue, with the continued rise in the work forces of state and local governments, government-oriented corporations, and private nonprofit institutions.

Long-range forecasting is an extremely hazardous occupation. Developments somewhat far in the future are subject to our control to a far greater degree than the events of tomorrow. The forecast itself may well set in motion influences that will prevent the achievement of the forecast. Nevertheless, it would seem that the prospect is for a mixed economy in the United States, but a far more intricate mixture than has been experienced thus far.

In the past, most discussions of this nature have simplistically assumed a clean dividing line between public and private. The very phrase "mixed economy" has mainly indicated that the line was not being drawn at either extreme, that both public and private production and consumption of goods and services were involved. For example, the Tennessee Valley Authority and the Pacific Gas and Electric Company both produce and distribute power, the former being a government agency and the latter a private corporation. The Post Office Department and the Railway Express Agency both deliver parcels; again, one is public and the other private.

The mixed economy that is now developing is different. It is characterized by mixed organizations, each of which possesses characteristics of both public institutions and private organizations. Hence, the modern public sector that is developing is hardly something aloof and entirely separate from the private sector; rather in its usual pragmatic fashion, the United States is fashioning policy tools not for the sake of their intrinsic beauty, but to achieve a growing variety of difficult and far-reaching national objectives.

With this turn of events, we no longer can adhere to the old-fashioned notion that the degree to which a country has become socialistic can simply be measured by whether the means of production are publicly rather than privately owned. A few examples may suffice.

Numerous private individuals and corporations operate hotels, restaurants, and other concessions in national parks and forests. When the structures are put up by the federal agency, the traditional concept would treat the operation as public. However, if the concessionaire owned the facility, the entire operation would then have to be considered private. The distinction appears to be both arbitrary and based on a relatively trivial criterion.

The design and production of weapon and space systems by private companies in government-owned facilities is an example that we have considered in detail and the public-private relationships are far more complicated than the mere ownership of physical assets. For more conventional activities the Post Office and other federal agencies lease buildings and major items of equipment from commercial sources, and the departments of Agriculture and Interior lease private land for the recreational facilities that they operate. Does the private ownership of these assets automatically convert the federal agencies using them into private instrumentalities? That would hardly appear to be the case.

Perhaps it is an exercise in futility to attempt to calibrate the exact degree to which a modern Western economy has become nationalized or socialized. Rather than measure the ownership of the means of production or the financing or purchase of the output of an economy such as ours, it may be more fruitful to consider the changing locus of decision-making. In a sense, the American society has perhaps unwittingly adopted simultaneously the two alternative approaches to decentralization which Professor Egon Neuberger has called "administrative" and "polycentric."[9] Administrative decentralization may be considered to occur when the central authority delegates some of its decision-making to lower levels of authority; however, it keeps the power to review the results and even to revoke the authority.

Polycentric decentralization involves the dispersal of decision-making power to independent decision-makers. In concept, the federal form of government and the private enterprise system would be considered polycentric. The use of the "tied" grant-in-aid and the government-oriented corporation, however, may occupy the vague no-man's land between the two forms of decentralization.

It would appear likely that in coming years increasing proportions of federal funds will be disbursed via state and local governments, intergovernmental agencies, government-oriented corporations, quasi-private institutions, and perhaps even newer organizations possessing both public and private characteristics. The typical federal agency indeed will probably be a policy formulator and program overseer dealing with operations decentralized in a variety of ways and over a wide span of the American economy. This would be a broader development than Peter Drucker's suggested decentralization of governmental operations. He would avoid reliance on state and local governments for the conduct of programs and would draw exclusively on the nongovernmental institutions of the society for the actual performance of public functions—hospitals, universities, business firms, labor unions, and other private organizations.[10] Hence, this study envisions that the federal government will not choose between the two routes of greater federalism or further involvement of the private sector, but that both paths of decentralization will be followed simultaneously.

The initiative for public activities may vary substantially among the different program areas. In some cases, such as highways, the states may exercise basic responsibility, with federal financial support. In others, local governments may continue to exercise leadership, education being an important example, with both federal and state agencies providing money and technical assistance. Research may be the area in which companies and agencies and even individuals represent the locus of entrepreneurship, and various public and nonprofit agencies support them.

This continual intertwining of public and private activities, although it would make difficult the technical tasks of measurement and analysis of the different sectors of the economy, may provide a very considerable strength and resiliency to American institutions during periods of substantial internal stress and strain.

NOTES

1. Monroe W. Karmin, "Housing the Poor," *Wall Street Journal,* February 5, 1969, p. 1.
2. U.S. Congress, House, Committee on Government Operations, *Pollution of Lake Michigan* (Washington, D.C.: U.S. Government Printing Office, 1967).
3. Murray L. Weidenbaum, "The Scope of Government Spending," *Western Political Quarterly,* XXXV, No. 2 (December 1960), 910–917; Lloyd D. Musolf, "Public Enterprise and Economic Planning: A Comparative Prospective," *George Washington Law Review* (December 1966), pp. 362–377.
4. "Federal National Mortgage Association," *Monthly Review of the Federal Reserve Bank of Richmond* (July 1968), pp. 2–5.
5. Arnold H. Diamond, "Changing Relationships Between the Public and the Private Sectors," *Proceedings of the Sixtieth Annual Conference on Taxation* (Pittsburgh: National Tax Association, 1967), pp. 112–129.

6. See U.S. Congress, Senate, Committee on Government Operations, *Government Competition with Private Enterprise* (Washington, D.C.: U.S. Government Printing Office, 1963).

7. See U.S. Bureau of the Budget, *Use of Management and Operating Contracts*, circular A–76, 1966.

8. Clarence H. Danhof, *Government Contracting and Technological Change* (Washington, D.C.: Brookings Institution, 1968), p. 112.

9. Professor Egon Neuberger, a lecture at Washington University on February 24, 1969. See also Frederic L. Pryor, *Public Expenditures in Communist and Capitalist Nations* (Homewood, Ill.: Richard D. Irwin, Inc., 1968), pp. 27, 437.

10. Peter F. Drucker "The Sickness of Government," *Public Interest*, No. 14 (Winter 1969), p. 17.

INDEX

acid mine drainage, 84
Ackley, Gardner, 19
Adams, Walter, 32
Adelman, Morris, 45–46
administrative decentralization, 198
Administrative Procedures Act, 51
Advisory Commission on Intergovernmental Relations, 121, 127
Aerojet-General Corporation, 78, 80, 84, 85, 88
aerospace companies, market diversification in (Table 3–1), 72
Aerospace Corporation, 97, 105
aerospace systems, 11–12, 48, 78, 79, 88
Agency for International Development, 81, 83
agricultural subsidies, 168–169, 180–181
Agriculture, Department of, 16, 174, 197
Air Force: development of new weapons systems for, 195; nonprofit organizations and, 104–106, 159; procurement, 40, 46
Air Force, Department of the, 20, 21

air pollution, 3, 6
Air Research and Development Command, 42
air transportation network, nationwide, 5
aircraft carriers, nuclear-powered, 8–9, 12
allocation of resources (*see* resource allocation)
allocative efficiency, 25–26
Aluminum Company of America, 55
American Cement Company, 88
American Telephone and Telegraph Company, 58
Analytic Services, Inc., 104
Anheuser-Busch, 35
annual income, guaranteed, 111–112, 128
anti-poverty program, 3, 5, 9, 10, 14, 88–89, 96, 98–100, 124, 169, 180
antitrust laws, 7
Appalachian Regional Commission, 93–95
appropriation bills, 156–157, 168, 172, 174–175